To our children:

Christian

Emily

Heather

Jennifer

Joel

Josie

Julia

Rose

William

The Peaceful Parenting Handbook

Burt Berlowe
Dr. Elizabeth Lonning
Dr. Joseph Cress

Resource Publications, Inc.
San Jose, California

Reprint Department
Resource Publications, Inc.
160 E. Virginia Street #290
San Jose, CA 95112-5876
1-408-286-8505 (voice)
1-408-287-8748 (fax)

Library of Congress Cataloging-in-Publication Data
Berlowe, Burt.
    The peaceful parenting handbook / Burt Berlowe, Elizabeth Lonning, Joseph Cress.
      p.   cm.
    ISBN 0-89390-513-5
    1. Child rearing. 2. Discipline of children. 3. Parenting. I. Lonning, Elizabeth, 1962– II. Cress, Joseph, 1944– III. Title.
    HQ769.B5188   2001
    649'.1—dc21   00-051724

Printed in the United States of America

01 02 03 04 05| 5 4 3 2 1

Editorial director: Nick Wagner
Editor: Kenneth Guentert
Production coordinator: Mike Sagara
Copyeditor: Robin Witkin

Contents

Acknowledgments   vii

Introduction: And How Are the Children?   1

Chapter One: Patterns of Daily Living   7

    Getting Up   7

    Getting Dressed   9

    Mealtime   11

    Keep It Clean: Personal Hygiene   14

    Bedtime   16

Chapter Two: Interpersonal Relationship Problems   21

    Sibling Problems   21

    Public Behavior   27

    Attention Seeking   31

    Peer Relationship Problems   38

    Aggression and Fighting   46

Chapter Three: Minding and Cooperation   53

    Compliance in General   53

    Responsibility   59

    Neatness   62

    Taking Care of Bedrooms and Personal Property   66

Chapter Four: Bad Habits   69

    Overcoming Bad Habits in General   69

    Thumb Sucking   71

    Nail Biting   72

    Lying   73

Swearing 78

Procrastination and Dawdling 80

Temper Tantrums 83

Spitting 86

Chapter Five: Emotional Problems **89**

Fears and Phobias 89

Soiling 94

Sadness 96

Dealing with Overdependency 101

Sleep Disturbance 104

Eating Disturbances 107

Chapter Six: Problems of Immaturity **113**

Bed Wetting 113

Misuse of Money and Allowances 116

Overly Active, Distractible,
and Inattentive Behavior 119

Manipulative Crying 124

Chapter Seven: School-Related Problems **127**

Balking at Going to School 127

Underachievement and Poor Study Habits 130

Truancy 138

Afterword: Beyond Discipline **143**

Acknowledgments

With out the support, encouragement, and involvement of many people, this book would not have been written. We would specifically like to acknowledge several people who have been instrumental. Kenneth Guentert, our editor, has provided encouragement and valuable advice. Julie Walker helped prepare many drafts of the manuscript. We are grateful to our spouses and children for their patience and support. Finally, we would like to thank the parents and children who have shared their experiences with us.

Introduction

And How Are the Children?

As we enter a new millennium with all of its hopes and challenges, one question should become of paramount importance in everyone's minds: How are the children?

To illustrate this point, we want to relate an old Native African tradition conveyed in a speech by Rev. Patrick T. O'Neill of the First Parish Unitarian Universalist Church in Farmington, Massachusetts:

> Among the most accomplished and fabled tribes in Africa, no tribe was considered to have warriors more fearsome or more intelligent than the mighty Masai. It is surprising, then, to learn the traditional greeting that passed between Masai warriors. "Kasserian ingers," one would always say to another. It means, "and how are the children?" It is a traditional greeting among the Masai, acknowledging the high value that the Masai always place on their children's well-being. Even warriors with no children of their own would always give the traditional answer, "all the children are well," meaning of course that peace and safety prevail, that the priorities of protecting the young, the powerless, are in place, that Masai society has not forgotten its reason for being is proper functions and responsibilities. "All the children are well" means that … the daily struggles of existence, even among poor people, do not preclude properly caring for its young ….

When we first published *Peaceful Parenting in a Violent World* in 1995, the answer to the Masai question left a lot to be desired historically and in current times. Children have been abused in one form or another since the beginning of civilization. Ancient Greeks and Romans commonly abused infants and young boys. Chinese girls traditionally had their feet bound to keep them graceful and sexually desirable. In many countries, children have long been treated as less than human, owned and herded like sheep or cattle, abandoned at an early age, or even sold into slavery. Over the last two millennia, there have been increasing waves of enlightenment and liberation in child rearing. Yet, child abuse incidents remain at an all-time high.

The twentieth century was the most violent in our history. Societal violence spiraled out of control, with children as the primary victims. Much of that violence occurred in the home. Despite increasing evidence of the harmful effects of physical and emotional abuse, parents have continued to spank, belittle, and neglect their children at alarming rates. At the end of the century, the response to the report card on the nation's children was a dismal one indeed. It could be safely said that our children were not doing very well at all.

The twentieth century was hard on parents, too. Most parents want to raise happy, well-adjusted, self-confident children, but that is a difficult task in our violent culture. Parents often think that they do not have the knowledge or skills necessary to raise their children in a world in which they face a constant bombardment of drive-by, schoolyard, and workplace shootings; gang wars; terrorism; growing domestic assaults; and a steady barrage of media violence. In addition, parents have to deal with the stresses of competition, exploitation, and alienation. The anger and frustration that originate at work (or en route) often find release at home. Using alcohol or drugs to relieve anxiety often precipitates family violence. Parenting itself is stressful. Parents are often tempted to react abusively to unacceptable childhood behavior. Frustrations in rearing children can lead even the gentlest parent to an occasional loss of control.

There are two primary reasons children are abused. One is lack of parenting knowledge. Without knowing alternative options, parents usually rear their children as they were raised—for better or worse. Parenting is the toughest job in the world. Few of us are automatically equipped to handle it, and we aren't given the tools when we first need them. Couples can learn the proper regimen for childbirth but nothing about what to do with the child once it is born. As a result they fall back on their own family or cultural experiences as the only reference point they know. It is a well-known fact that most people who were abused as children continue that cycle when they become parents. That's why having access to a wealth of options and the skill to use them is so critical to being a peaceful parent.

Although we offer many options for child rearing, we remain abundantly clear about one thing. *Child abuse is wrong,* and we must do everything we can to prevent it. That means a firm NO to all forms of abuse: physical, emotional, verbal, sexual, and—most common of all—neglect. That means no hitting, spanking, shoving, shaking, yelling, or put-downs. It also means giving children the most precious gift of all—time and attention. This book offers parents the opportunity to learn the nonviolent discipline skills they need to be peaceful parents.

The second primary cause of child abuse is the inability to manage anger. Abuse of any kind—physical, verbal, emotional—usually occurs in a fit of rage. By learning how to control and channel their anger, parents can usually avoid taking it out on their children. Managing anger is one of the seven habits of peaceful parenting addressed in our comprehensive parent training program and is the focus of the companion volume to this handbook.

But there is more to peaceful parenting than nonviolent discipline and anger control. The need to use consequences for misbehavior, for instance, can be reduced by preventing the misdeed in the first place. The best way to do that is through building and maintaining nurturing, caring, and consistent parent-child relationships that include ample quality time, meaningful communication, and democratic decision making.

We had all of this in mind when we wrote our first book on peaceful parenting and focused on nonviolent discipline strategies. We also featured information on the history, frequency, and impact of child abuse and on the peaceful parenting movement that is combating it. We viewed peaceful parenting as a holistic approach to child development that encompassed a variety of ways that all elements of society could use to raise peaceful children. In other words, we offered parents and other caregivers the opportunity to learn and practice the skills that would enable them to rear their children in a peaceful way.

The primary objective of our peaceful parenting book and the classes and workshops it has produced has been to arrive at the positive Masai answer—to help develop a next generation of citizens who would be more peaceful than those who have dominated the past century.

In the few years since we published our first book, we have met, talked with, and educated hundreds of parents from all kinds of families, cultures, and income levels—as well as day care providers, teachers, social workers, and others in the care-giving field. In various ways, we have continued to pose the question: "How are the children (doing now)?" Our contacts have evoked a variety of concerns and questions. But more often than not, their answer has been, in effect: "The children are still not well."

The opportunity to connect with the people who rear children has given us cause for both hope and despair. We are encouraged by the efforts of many parents and professionals who are practicing peaceful parenting and spreading the word to others.

Peaceful parenting events for families have been held throughout the Twin Cities of Minneapolis and St. Paul, Minnesota, precipitating the publication of a how-to manual on the subject by the Initiative for Violence Free Families. The publication of our book led to many opportunities for us to conduct parent education classes and workshops in a variety of settings and to participate in displays and speaking engagements at numerous conferences serving parents, educators, social workers, and other care providers. We have also established many constructive relationships with others in the field like Growing Communities for Peace, with whom we have shared resources, table space, project collaboration, and a warm growing friendship. Perhaps the most gratifying of our experiences with peaceful parenting has been the positive, often unsolicited feedback we receive from people who have read and used the book at home or in their professional setting.

At the same time, we are concerned about the pervasive violence in our culture, particularly against and by children. While recent surveys show an increased public awareness of the detriments of spanking, many parents still use it as their primary form of discipline and child abuse numbers continue to grow. Adults who have not yet heard or heeded the peaceful parenting message for one reason or another continue to abuse their children—sometimes with sticks or fists—often without lifting a finger.

Equally alarming is the way in which young people are turning that violence back on us. As this is being written, our nation is still reeling from a rash of schoolyard massacres that have driven home the need for better communication with our children. In discussion groups following these horrid events, the question always comes up: "Where were the parents?" A recent Minneapolis newspaper article reporting on one such meeting was headlined "Students Say Parents Key to Stopping the Violence." We don't know for sure whether the young perpetrators of the school crimes were victims of child abuse. However, it is obvious that they did not receive the kind of peaceful parenting at home or in the community that might have prevented their downfall into violence. What if these youngsters had learned some constructive ways to channel their anger and resolve their conflicts? What if they had been able to confide in a parent, teacher, or other caring adult about their deepest fears and frustrations? What if they had been reared with peacemaking skills? Could the result have been different?

As we begin a new century, we continue to believe that a holistic peaceful parenting philosophy can make a difference in mitigating violence. Children desperately need parental attention, nurturing, and proper modeling—however that can be done. The core of our philosophy still lies in nonviolent discipline, which by its nature teaches children right from wrong and fosters improved parent-child relationships.

In preparing this book, we followed the advice of our publisher and focused on the how-to element of peaceful parenting: the discipline strategies that will help you address common and uncommon childhood behavior problems in a peaceful way before they get out of hand, while creating an atmosphere of caring, concern, and meaningful communication that your children will carry with them out into a troubled world.

For the most part, these discipline techniques match those in our first book. However, we have made some key revisions in response to readers' concerns and the changing times. The reduced size and length of this book will make it easier to handle and read—an important factor in our busy, sound-bite culture—while still including the smorgasbord of alternatives that allow for flexibility and experimentation. We have also written a companion training manual for professionals and parents so others can continue and expand on the work we have begun. Whether or not you have already been exposed to peaceful parenting, we think you will find this format a handy way to improve your child-rearing skills.

We suggest the following sequence in using this book:

- Make sure you, as parents, agree on what childhood behavior needs to change. All involved parents need to be committed to the plan.

- Look up the targeted behavior in the table of contents. Review the relevant list of strategies.

- Identify those solutions most likely to work, taking into consideration child temperament, parenting styles, developmental status, and any other relevant variables. Make sure the plan is not too elaborate and can be maintained for weeks, even when you are tired and stressed.

- Stick with the plan for at least two to four weeks. Be very consistent. Remember, discipline is largely a trial-and-error process, and it is important to be flexible. If one solution doesn't work, another one will.

- Collect some very basic behavioral data before the plan is implemented and during the plan. This will help determine whether the plan is effective. Many times, parents think a plan is not working, when in fact it is.

- If after two to four weeks you don't see sufficient progress, try a new combination of solutions and go through the sequence again. Persistence and consistency will win out.

Rev. O'Neill continues in his speech:

I wonder how it might affect our consciousness of our children's welfare if, in our culture, we took to greeting each other with the same daily question: "And how are our children?" I wonder if we heard that question and passed it along to each other a dozen times a day, if it would begin to make a difference in the reality of how children are thought of or cared for in this country.

I wonder if every adult among us, parent and non-parent alike, felt an equal weight for the daily care and protection of all the children in our town, in our state, in our country .... I wonder if they could truly say without hesitation, "the children are well, yes, all the children are well."

Chapter One

Patterns of Daily Living

Getting Up

For many families, each day starts with stress. When it's time for children to get up, parents become tense and agitated as they anticipate conflicts. Some children don't get up after being called repeatedly. Or they stay in bed until the last possible minute. Meanwhile, parents fear the children will be late for school or church.

Depending on the circumstances surrounding problems with accomplishing daily tasks, these suggestions may help:

1. Ignore Bad Behavior

Examine your response to the getting-up process. Some parents unwittingly award privileges or treats to children who are tardy. For example, instead of having children prepare their own breakfasts, parents may do it for them. This kind of attention may only encourage a child's bad habits.

Instead, remove the reward. Let children make their own breakfasts, dress themselves, or face the consequences of arriving late at school. If these problems are handled in this way, procrastination will eventually subside.

2. Reward the Right Behavior

If a child gets up on time, then think about a reward. Material rewards, like a special breakfast treat, may help to get started. But it's important to be generous with social awards, such as praise and encouragement.

3. Allow for Natural Consequences

For school-age children, getting up is their responsibility, not yours. Teach children how to use an alarm clock. Let them help decide how much time to allow for washing, dressing, and eating in order to get to school on time.

If children oversleep, they must face the natural consequences: missing breakfast, dressing hurriedly, or walking instead of riding the bus to school. In using this approach, ask teachers or school officials for their support.

4. Go on Strike

With adolescents, parents should stay away from the morning ritual, remaining out of sight until the child has left for school. That way, the child has full responsibility for getting up, dressing, eating breakfast, and making it to school with lunch, books, and money in hand.

5. Rehearse

If children aren't in the habit of the morning routine, practice it during the day. Working together, a parent and child can set the alarm clock to ring in a minute or two. When the alarm goes off, the youngster shuts it off, gets up, and dresses. A variation of this strategy could be setting up the morning or bedtime routine or ritual like a relay race or an obstacle course. Younger children will find this a fun way to do tasks that are typically mundane or a hassle. Set up this strategy so that the tasks are thorough enough for the parents, yet enjoyable for the children.

6. Watch for Game Playing

The most elaborate plans for helping children assume responsibility for getting up on time can be sabotaged. For example, a sibling may slip into the room and awaken the child after the alarm has been turned off. When this happens, the child wins, and nothing is learned.

7. Use Conflict-Resolution Techniques

With older, more verbal children, various forms of conflict resolution can be of benefit. Allow children to suggest some solutions to the problem. These might shed light on their feelings about getting up late.

8. Respond Empathetically

Getting up in the morning is difficult for most people, and particularly for children. Youngsters find it hard to be alert and energetic at that time and are often grouchy. When that occurs, focus your response on the child's feelings rather than angrily decrying the procrastination. Comments like, "Boy, it's really hard to get up in the morning, isn't it?" or "Isn't it great just to lie in bed and dream?" can help create a bond of warmth and intimacy between parent and child.

9. Establish Routines

Children who have difficulty getting up on time in the morning may benefit from an established routine throughout the week, including the weekend. This means going to bed and getting up at the same time on Saturday and Sunday as during the week.

10. Check Out Hidden Conflicts

Children who fail to get up on time may be attempting to avoid something unpleasant, either at home, on the way to school, or at school. Some children are teased and hassled on the bus. Others have conflicts with certain instructors. Sometimes they want to avoid an aversive social situation. These conflicts must be checked out and dealt with.

11. Weed Out the Distractions

Many activities interfere with children falling asleep in a timely manner. They may have a radio or TV in their bedroom and don't turn it off until late at night. They may be listening to music past the curfew. Many teens like to chat on the phone with their friends until the wee hours of the morning. If there are distractions, they need to be eliminated to solve the morning rising problems.

12. Attach a Penalty

Children may have to get up earlier the next morning following a late rising. For example, if normal wake-up time is 7:00 A.M. but the children don't get up until 7:30 A.M., they might be told that the next morning they have to get up at 6:30 A.M. If they're fifteen minutes late, then they only have to get up fifteen minutes earlier the following morning.

Getting Dressed

Getting children dressed in the morning is another major hassle in many families. Children argue about which clothes to wear, refuse to dress themselves, and contribute to the risk of being late. Others dress and groom themselves hurriedly and haphazardly and don't look presentable.

The following suggestions may help in getting children dressed and ready for school or for the day:

1. Establish Consequences

Determine whether your child is indirectly receiving a reward by refusing to dress or by dressing improperly. If you give this behavior a lot of attention, you may be encouraging it. Consider using a chart to reward good behavior.

2. Practice

Again, rehearsals may be helpful. Young children may need to practice putting their clothes on the night before. This way, they become more adept at buttoning, snapping, and zipping.

3. Plan Ahead

Have children select their clothes the previous night. This eliminates decision making in the morning, leaving them with just the task of dressing. With younger children, it works best to give a choice of one of two outfits.

4. Use Logical Consequences

If your children can dress themselves, simply announce that you'll no longer help them. In defiance, a child may throw a tantrum or run around naked. To deal with this, take a change of clothing along in the car, and the child, if still in pajamas, can dress on the way to school.

5. Use Modeling

Parental modeling of appropriate dress is essential. Parents who wear clean appropriate clothes are more likely to have children who do the same. If children are careless about color coordination in their clothing choices, parents should pay attention to their own dress.

6. Ignore Criticism

Parents who use a natural- or logical-consequence approach must be prepared to deal with criticism. They may be seen as ineffective parents because of the way they dress their children. But dress is not an accurate reflection of parenting abilities. You don't need other people's approval to decide on a philosophy of discipline regarding dressing.

7. Be Reasonable

Parents of junior or senior high school youths need to understand that there are accepted dress codes, and there are social consequences of not dressing within the standards dictated by their peer group. Within reason, provide some stylish clothing to help your children fit in. But buying every piece of stylish clothing is far from necessary.

8. Ensure Clothing Comfort

Some children have difficulty getting dressed because of concerns about how the clothing feels on their skin. Some say the clothing itches or they will only wear certain materials or styles of clothing. Oftentimes, to combat these complaints, you can use "magic lotion," "anti-itch dust," or a more generic form, "comfort dust." Find a bottle that does not have any markings on it. Put a lotion or a powder in the bottle that becomes the "magic lotion," "anti-itch dust," or "comfort dust." Putting one of these products on the body parts that are uncomfortable, such as arms or legs, will relieve the discomfort and provide a protective barrier between the clothing and skin.

Oftentimes, this suggestion of increased comfort will take care of the complaints. Employ this paradoxical approach so that children have complete control over how much of the product they use and where they put it—of course, within reason and with safety precautions. Also remember they will be the only people who are able to "purchase" these products so children continue the belief that these products are special.

Mealtime

Mealtime should be an enjoyable time for families. But too often there are vicious power struggles. Mothers may threaten, cajole, and nag children to eat. They may feel they have to prepare two or three different courses to please the palates of family members.

Mealtime often is a painful and conflicting time for families. A number of strategies may alleviate some of these tensions.

1. Implement Grandma's Rule

First, the child must finish something he or she finds unpleasant. Then the reward is being allowed to do something he or she enjoys. For example, a child must eat the main course of a meal before getting dessert or a bedtime snack.

2. Establish Timing

In some families, it may be helpful to begin and end meals at certain times. If a child is late, he can continue to eat until the time is up. If she misses mealtime, she can't have a snack. But she is welcome to try again at the next scheduled meal.

3. Serve One Main Course

Homes are not restaurants. Don't serve a variety of main courses. If children don't like the main course, they can wait until the next meal, with no desserts or snacks in between.

4. Set a Good Example

Parents are the most influential models with respect to children's eating habits. Children can't be expected to show good manners if parents don't.

5. Allow Logical and Natural Consequences

Children should be allowed to serve themselves. If they fail to eat all of their food, what they leave can be saved for the next meal. Children who eat adequately at a main meal may be allowed to snack, providing they clean up after themselves. It's acceptable for children to refuse to eat meat or some other main dish, provided they eat other well-balanced meals. Studies have shown that over time, most children will eat a balanced and nutritious diet.

For children who decide to eat only one kind of food, offer to serve only that food and nothing else for every meal for several days. Usually, they'll quickly grow tired of that particular food and want something else.

6. Avoid Sabotage

Even though one parent might be successful in staying away from the power struggle regarding food, the other parent, a grandparent, or a sibling could undermine the whole plan. The cries of a hungry child melt the hearts of most grandparents.

If you are unable to control the behavior of another person in this regard, then try a different strategy. For example, parents who feel their efforts are being sabotaged might move from the dinner table. If siblings are the saboteurs, ask them to eat elsewhere until they change their ways.

7. Use Realistic Thinking

Significant mealtime problems can be eliminated if parents are able to identify their own unrealistic and self-defeating attitudes with respect to food. Parents, for example, may worry if children don't like all foods or don't always eat balanced meals. Parents with anxieties about their children's eating habits should examine their thinking. Just because children don't always eat right doesn't mean parents have failed.

8. Give Choices

Giving children a choice at each meal may nourish a sense of responsibility for their own behavior. You might ask, "Do you want eggs over easy or sunny-side up?" or "Do you want butter on your toast or not?" Some not terribly popular foods may be optional, but other foods are required.

9. Use Empathic Responding

When children complain about their food, don't view their complaints as opinions. Comments, if made at all, should focus on a child's feelings, without offering specific suggestions. For example, if a child complains that the soup is too hot, instead of offering a solution, say, "You'd like it a little cooler."

10. Establish Routines

Given the hectic schedules of contemporary families, carefully establish a mealtime routine that appears to fit the needs of most family members. As much as possible, this should be roughly at the same time every day. Snacks, if allowed, should also be at the same time of the day. Children who are difficult at mealtime might do better without snacks.

11. Reward Behavior

Appropriate mealtime behavior can be followed by a variety of potentially reinforcing consequences. One could be to allow the child to help with either meal selection or meal preparation the next time. Other appropriate mealtime rewards could include social rewards like hugs, kisses, and compliments, as well as additional privileges, including watching a few more minutes of TV or playing a favorite game with a parent.

12. Give the Cook a Vacation

Another strategy for mealtime difficulties is to have the cook take a vacation. For some parents, the kitchen becomes more like a short-order restaurant; in this respect, sometimes even short order cooks go on vacation. Before the cook goes on vacation, there should be sufficient supplies in the household so that other responsible members of the family or even the parent who does the least amount of cooking can take care of meals. Sometimes a paradoxical strategy such as this can shake up the routine enough around mealtime that children are far more reasonable about what they are willing to eat and the kinds of tasks they are willing to do to help prepare for mealtime. An extended vacation of up to a week may be needed to shake up the mealtime routine.

Keep It Clean: Personal Hygiene

Another problem that occurs in many families involves basic cleanliness. Children are hounded to brush their teeth and to wash their hands and faces. When parents are preoccupied with cleanliness, power struggles often emerge.

Here are some strategies for parents to use in enforcing personal hygiene.

1. Try a Behavioral Viewpoint
Since most hygienic behaviors are desirable, use a chart with relevant rewards to increase the frequency of self-care. By recognizing appropriate behavior and downplaying a lack of it, hygiene habits will most likely become automatic and continue into adolescence and adulthood.

2. Use a Hard-Nosed Approach
Although ruling over a child's personal appearance or hygiene habits is risky business, some parents make it a high priority. If that's the case, start early and explain exactly what your cleanliness standards are. When your expectations are not met, you can fairly pursue consequences like the loss of freedom and privileges.

3. Learn by Example
If parents expect children to groom themselves properly and show self-discipline in personal hygiene, they should model such behavior consistently. A father who comes to the table with grease on his hands or a mother who has yellow teeth are not setting suitable examples. In cleanliness, as in other areas, it's what the parents do, not what they say, that really counts.

4. Implement Grandma's Rule
In cases where children are chronically dirty, unkempt, or slovenly, you can set up a "first, then" program. In other words, "First, you wash your hands; then you can eat," or "First, you take a bath; then you can watch TV."

5. Try the There's-the-Door Approach
In cases of older adolescents who show delinquent tendencies, hard-nosed behaviorists recommend kicking them out if they re-

fuse to comply with parental hygiene standards. The message of this approach is, "Shape up or ship out." This is a severe tactic that can cause anxiety for the parent and anger and resentment for the child. Use it only if nothing else works.

6. Allow Natural and Logical Consequences

In this approach, children are allowed to choose whether they will bathe or not. After a while, the responses of family members and others may shame them into taking more interest in personal hygiene. At mealtime, for example, a child who has not bathed may be asked to sit elsewhere.

When it comes to brushing teeth, the issue usually should be between the child and the dentist. However, tell your child that if she doesn't brush her teeth, she won't get sweets. Meanwhile, give her brother who brushes his teeth sweets. For older children, another natural consequence approach is to make them pay their own dentist bill. In any case, don't nag. State the facts and let children decide when to improve their dental habits.

7. Establish Routines

Children who have difficulty with personal hygiene may benefit from established routines. Post an actual schedule with specified times and particular personal care behavior. For example, the schedule might indicate that at 7:00, they take a shower and wash their hair on Tuesday, Thursday, and Saturday. On Monday, Wednesday, and Friday, they wash their hair only—no shower. After breakfast, they brush their teeth and hair, and, if necessary, use deodorant. At 4:00, they may change from school clothes into play clothes. At 9:00, they may take a bath; otherwise, they wash their face and hands and brush their teeth.

8. Practice Makes Perfect

When children have difficulty with personal hygiene, tell them what the rules are and have them practice the activities of personal hygiene. They may need to be shown again how to take a shower, wash their hair, brush their teeth, and comb and brush their hair. This should not be done in a punitive or caustic manner, but very matter-of-factly, as though there's a deficiency in their knowledge base, and they need some extra help—just as they might need extra help in reviewing how to do a complex multiplication problem with fractions.

9. Reward Good Behavior

Certainly, social rewards like hugs, kisses, and compliments are important. Additional privileges are also helpful. Some chronic culprits benefit from a written contract. In a contract, list the specified personal hygiene behaviors and specify rewards. The contract is then signed by both the parents and the child.

10. Use the Pigpen Analogy

An analogy to the cartoon character Pigpen from the *Peanuts* comic strip can help children recognize what they may look or smell like if they choose not to exercise their daily hygiene skills. Seek out books with the comic strip characters and look for some strips that contain scenes with Pigpen to get an idea of how the kids are treating Pigpen. This may be a way to mimic treatment of the child who does not engage in daily hygiene in the family.

Bedtime

The cycle of ordinary problems in many families reaches a climax at bedtime. Children squabble about the time they are to go to bed. Once in bed, they demand drinks, ask to go to the bathroom, or nag parents to sleep with them.

There are a number of ways to deal with problems involving bedtime.

1. Establish a Reward

Specify going to bed on time without disruptions as an item on a chart, and reward appropriate behavior the following morning. Ignore disruptive conduct by refusing to respond to a child's pleas or closing yourself in your bedroom.

2. Define Territorial Rights

Many parents innocently allow children to sleep with them during a storm, or when youngsters are upset. Slowly but surely, children refuse to return to their own beds.

Behaviorists suggest two approaches for dealing with this problem. Some encourage locking either the children's or the parents' bedroom door. This can result in anxiety, fright, and turmoil that may persist for a few days. But in time, the child will learn that sleeping alone is not threatening.

Another approach works more slowly. Gradually move the child farther and farther from your bed. First, tell the child your bed is off limits. The child must sleep on the floor in a sleeping bag in your room, for example. If you wake up and find the child in your bed, put the child back on the floor. After a week or so, move the sleeping bag two to four inches closer to the doorway. Repeat this process until the sleeping bag is back in the child's own room.

3. Set an Example
It's important that parents set appropriate models for regular bedtime and rising times. This will help the child establish a similar routine.

4. Establish a Ritual
Bedtime rituals started when a child is a toddler can continue into adolescence. Begin the routine at the same time every night. It could include a bath followed by stories or a snack. Remember that you can make children go to their bedrooms, but you can't make them fall asleep.

5. Be Realistic
Parents who become unnecessarily preoccupied with the sleep issue and worry about the amount of rest their children receive only encourage problems. Over time, children usually get as much sleep as they need. If there are significant indications of sleep disturbance, pursue professional consultation.

6. Allow Logical and Natural Consequences
Tell children that you need time to yourselves and that they must be in bed by a certain time. If children get up after bedtime, firmly but silently put them back in their rooms. In dealing with older children, ostracize them when they refuse to go to bed. Everyone else should retire, leaving the children to either sleep where they are or go back to their rooms. In most cases, children will soon learn to abide by the rules.

Another logical consequence strategy is to say that at a certain time, children should be ready for bed. If they aren't ready by that time, they should be sent to bed anyway, wearing whatever clothes they have on.

7. Use a Child-Centered Approach
A more protective and permissive strategy is to set flexible bedtime hours, letting children decide when to go to bed within a certain time frame, such as between 8:00 and 9:00. If children demand attention after that time, approach them in an empathic manner, ac-

knowledging that they would like to stay up longer but that the limits hold.

Establishing a ritual can make bedtime an intimate and personal time for children and parents to share. The empathic approach also recommends that discussion about bedtime be done passively. For example, rather than "You have to go to bed," simply say, "It's bedtime."

8. Establish a Bedtime Routine

Children who have difficulty going to bed or getting up on time may need routines. If necessary, the bedtime routine should be consistent and followed every night, including weekends.

9. Weed Out Any Distractions

Prevent children from becoming overly excited or stimulated before bedtime. By the same token, begin calming and quieting activities at least an hour to a half-hour before bedtime. Eliminate TV, phone calls, caffeinated drinks, and roughhousing well before bedtime. Also, children shouldn't nap after dinner. Quiet activities could include listening to soft music, taking a bath, or being read a story.

10. Help Them Go to Sleep

Even when children get to bed on time, they don't always fall asleep on the time schedule that parents might like. As a preventive measure, don't bring up upsetting topics during quiet time before bed. Some children might find it helpful to read a relatively boring book in bed. Sometimes, quiet instrumental music helps children fall asleep. Remember that children who are not fully asleep but are quietly resting may wake up reasonably refreshed and alert the following morning.

11. Allay Their Fears

Some children have a difficult time going to sleep because they are concerned about monsters or other scary creatures entering their bedroom and keeping them awake. A product that parents can create to help with this is something along the lines of "Witch Be Gone" or "Monster Be Gone." In effect, parents create this product by getting a generic unmarked container. Fill it with water, some vinegar or other strong-smelling kitchen product, and a combination of food coloring so that it looks ominous and smells terrible. The key ingredients to this product are that it smells awful and looks potent. Make sure the bottle has a spray nozzle so that children are able to spray it wherever they are concerned a witch or monster may reside.

As with the comfort products discussed in the clothing section, children need to be able to control where this product is sprayed and how much of it is used. In this respect, the product needs to consist of ingredients that are not going to damage furniture or fabrics in a child's room. Tell the child that this is a very powerful spray, that only parents are allowed to purchase it, and that he needs to be careful in using it because it will take care of monsters, witches, or any other creature that the child may be concerned about. Giving children control over their fear can eliminate the fear itself.

A slight variation is when a child is afraid to go to sleep because she may have bad dreams. It often helps to have a dream catcher. A dream catcher can be made out of anything, even a paper bag from the grocery store. It does not have to be as elaborate as the Native American dream catchers sold commercially. The dream catcher needs to come with specific instructions. It should be hung above the child's head, and it needs to be emptied regularly so that the bad dreams can float away.

Chapter Two

Interpersonal Relationship Problems

Problems that involve interactions and relationships among family members can be distressing. These situations are most difficult to handle when they occur in public. For example, a grouchy or irritable child can keep the whole family in turmoil. Sibling differences and quarrels can lead to unhappy family relationships. Some children who feel cheated within the family circle constantly seek special attention. In fact, they may seem to have an insatiable need for admiration and affection.

As children grow, peer relationship problems emerge. The influence of the peer group often leads a child to borderline or actual antisocial behavior toward the family. Other children are never fully accepted by any peer group and, as a result, feel shy or unworthy.

Sibling Problems

Sibling fighting occurs in almost every family with two or more children. When parents complete behavior problem checklists indicating their concerns, almost invariably they mention sibling quarrels as a significant and recurrent problem. Sibling fighting usually results from one of two causes. The usual reason is seeking parental attention. Another reason is low frustration tolerance.

To deal with sibling fighting, consider the following strategies.

1. Try Extinction
When children fight for parental attention, try leaving the scene of the bickering and retiring to the bathroom. This course of action is recommended only if the motivation for the fighting is attention-seeking and if there is no danger of physical injury to the children.

When the fighting has subsided for a few minutes, return to the scene in silence. If it erupts again, repeat the procedure. A less dramatic version is to remain in the same room as the children but ignore the fighting.

2. Use Modeling

Many children who tease, provoke, and irritate siblings learn these undesirable habits from their parents. For example, if a parent constantly nags and criticizes a child, it won't be long before children will do the same thing to each other.

Another frequently occurring situation is bullying and picking fights. Children learn to be bullies and instigators from other people, particularly their parents. For instance, parents may tell children to stand up for themselves and not let anyone boss them around. Some children interpret that advice loosely. Whenever something doesn't go their way, they believe they should defend themselves by fighting.

3. Allow Consequences

Sibling fighting is complicated. Often, there is more than one culprit. Consequently, if you are using consequences, penalize both children. The most obvious and straightforward strategy is to put each of the battlers in isolation for one minute for each year of the child's age. At that point, tack on another consequence: "If you fight again, neither of you will be able to watch TV for the rest of the day."

Isolation can be an important way of dealing with fighting because it offers children a chance to cool off and think about the reasons for their actions, as well as the possible consequences if their misbehavior continues. After the isolation period, the time is right to discuss some alternative ways of solving the problem.

4. Give Rewards

In most families, fighting continues because it offers ample bonuses, like attention from parents. In certain situations, parents should reward children for cutting down on their fighting. Give children who quit fighting special privileges or material and social awards.

5. Try Alternative Problem Solving

With older, more articulate children, problem-solving strategies can be helpful. Once the problem has been identified, ask children to do some brainstorming to come up with ways to resolve the issue, and then weigh the pros and cons of each proposed solution. This strategy should be used after a cooling-off period, not when tempers are flaring.

6. Use Role Reversal

After the enraged children have calmed down, ask them to switch roles with each other. This requires ten to twenty minutes for the children to play a game as actors or actresses pretending to be each other. For example, Jason will play Jane, and Jane will play Jason. With the parent as director, children re-enact the fighting scene, playing the opposite part. They should engage in two or three interactions. If the dialogue results in excessive insults or name-calling, it may have to be stopped, reviewed, and started again. Afterward, sit down with the children and ask them how they felt in their reversed roles, especially when they were attacked by the person who took on their identity. This strategy can help enhance empathy and increase self-control, a trait required in role reversal.

7. Police Filmed Violence

Psychological studies increasingly show that children's attitudes toward aggression and violence are strongly influenced by movies and TV. Children who view brutality are likely to become brutal.

8. Examine Your Attitudes

When children fight, parents often overreact. Such attitudes include, "I can't stand fighting," or "If my kids fight, they'll grow up to be criminals." Other exaggerated thoughts might be, "I'm a rotten parent and a failure because my children fight."

To change this self-defeating thinking, identify your unrealistic attitudes, challenge and debate them, and eventually replace them with healthier alternatives. More realistic attitudes include: "I don't like the fighting but I can stand it," "I wish that they could cooperate and get along better, but it's not a big deal," "Even though I didn't handle this particular incident perfectly, it doesn't mean I'm no good as a parent," or "Criticizing myself won't help them stop fighting anyway."

9. Teach Morality

Young children can't easily understand the moral issues involved in sibling fighting. But older children may have the ability to change their behavior because they can comprehend how their actions can hurt others. They may respond to a more logical and realistic discussion of the meaning and consequences of aggressive behavior.

10. Stress Cooperation

It's difficult for children to fight and cooperate at the same time. Accordingly, fighting can be decreased if cooperation is increased. Encourage and reward cooperative and constructive behaviors like doing chores and household projects.

11. Display Empathy

An empathic approach may help children identify their feelings. This approach could include statements like "You're having fun bickering and enjoy getting my attention. You'd like me to come and solve your problem." Then make it clear to the child how this problem is going to be resolved. For example, "That's not the way things are done around here. If you continue fighting, there'll be no snack this afternoon."

12. Use Expulsion

Older bickering children can simply be asked to leave the house and go to the backyard. You might say, "If you continue fighting, you must go outside. When you're finished, then you can come back in." If the fighting continues, escort the children outside in complete silence and lock the door. When the bickering stops, they may return, but don't comment. This method has the greatest likelihood for success if parental attention-seeking is the motivation for fighting.

13. Handle Fights in the Car

Many parents feel helpless in dealing with fights in the car, but a number of strategies may help. Stop the car and get out, taking the keys along, stand near the car, and avoid looking at the children inside. When the fighting stops, get back inside and drive off without saying a word. If it's a particularly cold day, stay inside and order the children out of the car until they stop fighting.

14. Anticipate Problems

Parents who anticipate sibling rivalry can take steps to prevent hostility and jealousy from becoming frequent and intense. Sibling rivalry is most intense in families where children are of the same sex and in middle-childhood years. Remember that each child has a different temperament and personality, different strengths and weaknesses, and each should be dealt with individually.

Children also need to learn respect for each other's privacy and property. And although it may be convenient to have older children take care of younger ones, doing it excessively can foster resentment. It's primarily your job to oversee children.

15. Teach Assertiveness

Children can learn to stand up for their own rights and avoid arguments and fights by practicing assertive responses to use in given situations. For example, if they're bullied by an older sibling, they can learn to say, "I don't like it when you hit me. If you don't stop and play cooperatively, I'm going elsewhere."

16. Use Group Rewards and Consequences

Many teachers find it necessary to punish an entire class for disruption because it's impossible to figure out who's responsible for some act of misconduct. Similar situations may occur at home when it will be difficult to know who perpetrated a particular incident or egged on the troublemaker.

When this situation arises, announce that cooperative behavior will be rewarded by group incentives and uncooperative conduct by mass consequences. This way, the blame is fixed on no one individual. Follow cooperative behavior before mealtime by a special dessert. But if bickering occurs, announce that there will be no dessert and a loss of TV privileges for everyone involved.

17. Allow Anger

Although many parents grew up in the era that emphasized the suppression of negative feelings, letting anger and hostility out is, at times, healthy and productive.

Teach children that negative feelings are acceptable but that acting them out in fits of rage is not. Try giving the child a substitute means of expression. For example, a jealous child can be given a pillow to spank or hit. Also, children can release their hostility by creating drawings with vivid and dramatic colors.

18. Write It Down

Some child psychologists suggest that in cases of intense sibling conflict among older children, parents ask each child to write a report of one hundred or so words describing how the conflict started and grew, what it was about, and a recommendation for how a similar situation can be avoided the next time. In using this method, make up appropriate forms and run off copies. Then when fighting occurs, have the children fill out the forms. This particular consequence has educational and punitive aspects. After a few times, most children will avoid conflict to avoid writing a long report.

19. Use Bibliotherapy

Children who have difficulty getting along with each other can gain encouragement and ideas by identifying with a cooperative character in a story of legend. They begin to see similarities between themselves and the hero or heroine of the tale. In their own mind, they say, "She and I are alike. She handled her problems and I can handle mine."

20. Ask for Examples

If a child mentions that a parent favors one sibling, ask for a concrete example of the alleged unfairness. Don't use the word "why?" because that can trigger defensiveness. But say, "Let me see if you can tell me exactly what it was that made you feel that I treated Jimmy more favorably that you." Children often think in vague generalities, and their rationale for jealousy may be unfounded.

21. Keep a Diary

Children who chronically complain that they're victims of unfairness, favoritism, and partiality may be helped by keeping a diary in which they make a note of every perceived incident. Then they can discuss the situation with a parent. Gradually, the number of entries in the diary is likely to decrease.

22. Give Limited Responsibilities

Some children react adversely if they're given a parental role with regard to their younger siblings. Many older children aren't ready to routinely feed, dress, bathe, and supervise younger ones. Instead, give the older siblings important responsibilities for limited periods, such as teaching the younger sibling a new skill—how to play a game, tell time, or learn a new sport.

23. Give Positive Attention

When siblings compete intensively among each other, one-on-one, high-quality time may be helpful. Pick a time interval from ten to twenty minutes to be alone with each child. During that time, make the activities totally child directed unless major violations occur. Give the child the opportunity to set the tone and pick the games and activities. Don't give directions or be a disciplinarian; merely focus on interactions and the quality of the relationship.

24. Provide a Sanctuary

Each child needs a personal and private place in the house. It may be difficult for children who have to share a bedroom to find such a spot. Perhaps they could choose a special chair in their parents' bedroom or the dining room as their getaway. Accordingly, when they feel frustrated, imposed on, or hassled by siblings, they can retire to their sanctuary, and their request for privacy will be respected by all. This is not a site for punishment, but a haven for voluntary solitude and quiet.

25. Videotape or Audiotape the Fight

When children are fighting with one another, ask them to put their fight on hold for just a moment so that you can get the videocamera or the tape recorder. Tell them you want to record the events for posterity and add them to the family collection of videotapes or audiotapes to share with other family members or friends when they come to visit. Most children are not going to "perform" as they had originally thought they would when they know they are going to be recorded. If you can anticipate times in the future when children may be arguing, say things like, "Wait a minute, hang on. I need to go get the camera. Please wait until I can record this for the future." This may discontinue the sibling disagreement before it really gets fired up.

26. Be a Lawyer

Another strategy is to get children to think of the metaphor of a courtroom. Each child becomes a lawyer defending his or her position. This means they cannot fight amongst each other or the "judge" (parent) will throw them both out of the courtroom. Then instruct each child to go to a quiet place, maybe the bedroom, and actually create logical, calm, rational arguments for the decision to be made in his or her favor. At the end of this time, some children will have arguments to defend their position while others won't.

Public Behavior

A child who's well behaved at home can become a monster at the supermarket or in a restaurant. This can cause such embarrassment to parents that they lower their demands or expectations so the child won't cause a public scene. They may bribe or plead with the child and lose control of the situation.

Parents don't have to feel powerless in public. In trying to manage the unruly child in public, don't try disciplinary strategies that haven't been perfected at home.

The following effective strategies for bringing the child's public behavior into compliance may be helpful.

1. Employ Double Jeopardy

Assuming that you use isolation as a consequence at home, tell children that if they don't behave in public, they'll do double isolation time when the family returns. Some parents use a card. When misbehavior occurs in public, they calmly mark an X on the card or punch a hole in it. When they return home, they show the card to the child, who knows that every X or punch mark means double isolation time.

2. Enforce Grandma's Rule

A reward can help foster cooperation in public. Tell children beforehand that a special privilege awaits them if a public outing takes place without a disturbance. The reward doesn't have to be anything significant, and it's best to supplement it with compliments and encouragement.

3. Use Modeling

The example set by parents is paramount in the acquisition of appropriate public behavior. If parents throw temper tantrums in public, swear, or become easily upset with careless drivers or pushy shoppers, their children are likely to imitate that behavior. When parents exercise consistently smooth social interactions and are polite and courteous, they can expect their children to follow in those footsteps.

4. Try Role-Playing

Being in public can be uncomfortable and awkward for children and adults. Children may feel uneasy at a wedding reception or in a restaurant or church. Help your youngsters prepare for these social events by role-playing. For example, the family could act out going to the restaurant, with a parent in the role of a waiter or waitress. Children can practice ordering from the menu and mentioning a problem to a waiter if dissatisfied. Children can also benefit from practicing appropriate behavior in church, or rehearsing how they should conduct themselves at a wedding reception or family reunion.

5. Use Constructive Monologue

When parents experience upsetting public encounters, they may become excessively dismayed. They may think their kids are totally wild and undisciplined. "I don't see how we can ever go out in public or accept invitations to go anywhere," they may say. Or "It's so embarrassing when they misbehave in public. I can't stand it anymore."

Replace negative thoughts with constructive ones. "It certainly is embarrassing when my children act up in public, but it's not the end of the world. Their behavior doesn't mean we're rotten or ineffective parents. Perhaps some changes can be made that will help this problem."

6. Employ the Exit Technique

An effective strategy in dealing with public misbehavior is simply to leave the place where it's occurring. This works especially well when both parents are present. If the family is eating in a restaurant and the children act up, the whole family can leave. Or one parent can take the children out to the car and sit with them in silence while the other parent finishes eating. Then the parents can switch places so the other can finish the meal. This way, parents can eat with minimal disturbance, and children learn that disruptive behavior in restaurants is not tolerated.

If a child acts up during a shopping trip, take the disruptive youngster to the car, where they wait silently until the misbehavior stops, and then return to the store. Or take the child home, leaving the shopping cart and its contents behind.

The exit program works best in situations in which children are clamoring for parents' attention and when they have positive feelings about the outing.

Here is a slight modification for older children who decide to throw a temper tantrum in a public place. Simply walk on ahead and leave the child to tantrum alone. In most cases, they will soon tag along. If that doesn't happen, observe from around a corner to make sure the child is okay. When the child begins to look around for the parent, take it as a sign that the battle is won.

7. Progress Slowly

In preparing a child for public outings, proceed slowly and in an experimental fashion. Don't take children on a two-week cruise for their first public outing. Experiment with situations in which failures won't be disastrous or expensive and consequences can be applied decisively and with a high probability of success.

For example, start by visiting friends and relatives with whom you have conferred ahead of time. If a child is disruptive during the visit, the visiting family should leave quite abruptly.

8. Plan Ahead

When visiting friends or relatives, talk with the hosts and arrange for an area that could be used for isolation. Some stores even have out-of-the-way corners that might suffice. This type of preparation can be especially beneficial when visiting grandparents. Most children feel indulged by their grandparents, who may undermine parental power. By using customary disciplinary procedures, parents can minimize the distress of these visits.

9. Mold Polite Behavior

Parents want their children to be polite and courteous in public, and are embarrassed when this doesn't happen. Courtesy is learned by imitating other people, and the primary avenue for molding polite behavior is through example.

After going through an uncomfortable social situation, assume roles and rehearse the situation to find a more comfortable solution. Next time, the children will cope more confidently.

In practicing, suggest that children play the parts of not only real-life models, but also positive TV or movie characters. Polite behavior should be followed by positive feedback; for example, "Jimmy, thank you very much for introducing yourself in such a mature way." Impolite behavior should be ignored.

10. Review the Rules

When you are out in public, show children posted rules, read them, and demonstrate how they're to be followed. If rules aren't posted, ask the employees of the public places to identify what the rules are. Prior to entering, have the child repeat the rules. Then review the consequences. If the rules are followed, there'll be timely rewards. If they aren't, the public outing may be cut short and there may be a loss of privilege or isolation at home.

11. Deal with Bad Manners in Public

Manners have a lower priority than rules. Nevertheless, older children who burp, pass gas, pick their noses, or chew food with their mouths open are sources of distraction and embarrassment. Ignore mild cases of inappropriate manners, since they're often attention-seeking in nature. Or try a brief isolation period. Sometimes, nonverbal reminders such as frowns will nip bad manners in the bud.

12. Talk As-If

Another way to improve public behavior is to talk as if you are not sure what your child is doing or what they are trying to accomplish. Don't talk to the children directly but be sure they are listening. Speak to a cashier or to no one in particular, or muse out loud. You might say, "I wonder whose child is behaving this way," or "I am certain Johnny knows how to behave in a public place so this could certainly not be the Johnny I know," or "I sure hope that whatever that noise is that is making my shopping experience unpleasant today quits pretty soon or I am just going to have to leave."

Attention Seeking

Children have an insatiable need for attention. Understanding this need is critical for parents. A child has not only a need, but also a right to proper consideration, and the child and parent together must determine what's appropriate and inappropriate. Parents may have difficulty helping a child understand when it is time to get attention.

Children who don't get attention through proper means learn destructive, intrusive, and provocative ways to gain it. Meeting this need should be a high parental priority. Consider the following attention-related solutions.

1. Give Positive Attention

Before establishing strategies for reducing inappropriate attention-seeking behavior, determine whether your child is getting sufficient attention. The old dictum that a child is to be seen and not heard isn't true in every situation. Children are curious and adventuresome. They need the security of knowing they're cared for and protected by a loving parent. Learn to engage in activities that focus on what the child is doing, thinking, saying, and feeling.

One strategy calls for setting aside at least fifteen to twenty minutes each day, during which time the child chooses to play with something. Calmly sit or stand next to the child and carefully observe what he is doing, then begin to describe it objectively, with no questions or commands unless he becomes unruly. For instance, you might say, "I really like it when you and I sit together and play quietly."

As long as he plays appropriately, give him undivided attention. If noncompliant behavior occurs, turn away and attend to something else in the room. If the misbehavior continues, leave the room and conclude the attention-paying episode. This should be done daily so that the child receives at least a minimal amount of attention from each parent.

2. Ignore Bad Behavior

Most inappropriate attention-seeking behavior can be dealt with effectively by simply ignoring it. If the purpose of the behavior is to gain attention, it'll decrease in frequency if that goal isn't met. Most parents, however, have problems doing this consistently. If you choose to use this technique, do so without exceptions. To give in and ultimately pay attention is to tell the child that if she persists long enough, she'll get her way.

While ignoring seems easy, it's actually one of the most difficult strategies. However, if done properly and consistently, it will work virtually every time. This approach can be undermined when a child's other caretakers or friends don't use it. But even so, the child can learn that in the presence of a parent, the behavior is useless.

3. Cope with Back Talk

Back talk is an abrasive, irritating form of attention-seeking. It's important for parents not to respond to a child's back talk. Usually, back talk isn't the result of hatred or anger, but of the need for attention. The parent can simply ignore it. This is more difficult in dealing with teenagers than younger children because adolescents have better verbal skills and can use more provocative language. Sometimes it may be necessary to just leave the area, especially if the child is gaining control of the situation.

4. Handle Incessant Questions

Many parents comment that as soon as they begin talking with someone, their child begins a litany of "why" and "what" questions. This type of attention-seeking behavior can be difficult to deal with because it breaks no rules. The child, under the guise of seeking information, is demanding complete parental attention.

To punish such behavior may seem harsh because it is stifling the child's curiosity and desire to learn. But if these questions occur only in certain social situations and not when the parent and child are alone, it's evident that the motivation is not acquiring knowledge but gaining attention. In these cases, simply inform the child that this isn't the proper time to ask such questions. If this behavior persists, then either the child should be isolated or the parent and guest should leave the area.

These kinds of interruptions may also occur when the parent is talking on the telephone. To deal with this, discuss the situation with a friend and, when that friend calls, use a code word that means in essence, "Sally is being intrusive again, and I'm going to continue to talk to you while I ignore her. But I want you to hang up because I won't be able to listen to you and talk intelligently while ignoring her." Or simply pretend to be talking with someone on the phone. If these methods are used persistently, the child will soon learn that inappropriate attention-seeking won't be rewarded.

5. Contend with Constant Chatter

Precocious and verbal preschoolers often develop a knack for inappropriate attention-seeking behavior because of their newfound verbal skills. They begin babbling incessantly and soon gather a captive adult audience. Adults may feel awkward about ignoring the child. So they pretend to be interested while the child rants on and on.

This verbal rambling can result in the child talking about things that are highly private or inappropriate. If this happens, instruct other adults to ignore the child, perhaps by turning their backs on him or walking away.

6. Cope with Stealing

Some children openly and defiantly steal, knowing they'll get caught. Although attention-seeking stealing in preschoolers isn't criminal, it can become a serious problem. The excitement of the stealth can in time become rewarding and lead to increased activity. It's imperative to stop this behavior.

Ignoring it may not be effective in this case because the child may steal from people who won't consistently use this strategy. A loss of privilege or penalty might be a better method of discipline. In addition, use a reward system for improved behavior.

7. Handle Lying

Some children with a high need for attention tell elaborate false stories. For instance, a youngster may brag that she beat up four other kids at school, when no such incident occurred. Naturally, children receive a lot of attention from others when they tell these fantastic tales.

Don't overreact to this behavior. It doesn't mean that children can't distinguish reality from fantasy. However, you should be concerned enough to take appropriate action. In his book *Keeping Kids out of Trouble*, Dr. Dan Kiley suggests some logical consequences occur as a result of the child's fabrication ([New York: Warner Books, 1978], 137–141).

If the child talks about beating up other kids at school, say, "Because you have so much strength and energy, I want you to do three times as many chores as usual."

8. Overcome the Silent Treatment

Some children learn they can get as much attention by refusing to speak as they can by talking incessantly. If allowed to go to an extreme, this can develop into a pathological condition known as selective mutism. In these cases, the child refuses to talk at all in many situations, especially at school. This condition usually requires professional intervention. Most children will use strategies of a less severe nature, discovering that when they shrug their shoulders or give a curt response, they get all kinds of adult attention from parents trying to determine what's wrong with them.

Ignoring such behavior can turn it around quickly, particularly if you use it in relation to specific privileges. For example, ask your children what they want for dinner. If they don't answer, they get nothing. Or ask them whether they want to go to a movie or get a pizza. If they don't respond, they get neither. Usually, that kind of strategy will result in the child abandoning the use of silence as an attention-seeking ploy.

9. Deal with Daredevil Behavior

This can be a terrifying form of attention-seeking behavior. The child might climb to the top of the jungle gym and hang with one hand, for instance. This will naturally attract a parent's attention, which will encourage more of the same. If you are unable to turn your back on such behavior for safety reasons, stay away from those kinds of situations while the youngster is in that frame of mind. Or simply take the child home as soon as he or she engages in daredevil behavior.

10. Manage Argumentativeness

Arguing is a common form of attention-seeking behavior. It usually occurs when children want people to listen and pay attention to them. One way to deal with arguments is to have the child write them down before voicing them. In reviewing the written arguments, comment on the logic and the judgment the child shows, but not on winning or losing.

In giving the child feedback on the written argument, carefully point out that a good strategy in arguing is to agree at least in part with the other person. You might say, "In writing your arguments, be sure to indicate the things you agree on, too."

11. Try the Mimicking Treatment

Sometimes it's possible to have the whole family engage in the attention-seeking behavior of one of the children. For example, if a child is a whiner, say, "Okay, let's all whine just as loud as we can." If a child gains attention by being a slowpoke, say, "Okay, let's all of us be real slow, poke around and do everything in slow motion."

It's important not to dwell on this strategy. As soon as the family has engaged in it for a few minutes, they should abruptly change their activity and move on to something else without comment.

12. Reframe the Behavior

Depending on the nature of the attention-seeking behavior, it may be possible to approach the child seriously and say, "Jimmy, I've always wanted to know how to make that kind of noise. Show me how to do it. Then maybe you can teach all of us how to do it." If you use this technique, don't dwell on it. Do it quickly and decisively so as not to embarrass the child too much.

13. Praise the Child

Praise the child for something that has absolutely nothing to do with the child's attention-seeking behavior. For example, during some acting-out episode after dinner, say, "Jimmy, I really appreciate the way you took your dishes to the sink." Or while the child is seeking attention during a car trip, counter with, "Sally, I was really pleased with the way you cleaned up your room today." This seemingly irrelevant praising catches most children off guard and leaves them confused. It's often sufficient to end the pattern of attention-seeking behavior.

14. Deal with Tattlers

For some children, the rejection and scorn they get from siblings is minimal compared to the payoff they get from their parents for tattling. Most tattlers feel unnoticed, insecure, unappreciated, and often lonely. The goal of their behavior is the attentive response of an adult.

One option is to point out the consequences of a child's tattling behavior. For example, "Jimmy, while you were tattling on Jane, you missed a chance to see one of your favorite cartoons." Another idea is to reward the child for not tattling and to ignore or express disapproval when tattling occurs.

Still another choice is to change the subject when the tattler approaches. Most parents know in advance when a child is about to tattle and can preempt it by jointly agreeing to turn their attention to something different that will distract the child.

Role-playing with role reversal can also be an effective strategy in reducing tattling. When children feel what it's like to be the person tattled on, they may be less inclined to tattle again.

15. Deal with Teasing

Teasing can range from good-natured admiration to brutality that results in hurt feelings and bruised egos. If one child tends to be the target of most of the teasing, help that child decide what to do when the teasing begins. One possibility is to walk away. A second is to stare the person down without saying a word. A third option is discussing the behavior in a family meeting. A fourth is to confine the teaser and the victim to a room, telling them they must discuss their problem and find a solution before they can leave. With younger children especially, this sort of formal situation without direct parental supervision can result in quick problem solving.

Role-reversal may also be helpful. The child who was teased does the teasing and vice versa.

16. Cope with the Moaner, Groaner, and Griper

A child who complains chronically is usually unhappy, insecure, and in need of attention. This behavior isn't innate. A child learns it by imitating someone at home, at school, or in the neighborhood. One strategy is to eliminate the undesirable model.

Another strategy is to forbid all verbal moaning and groaning, insisting instead that it be done in writing. It may be helpful to have the child identify something positive with each complaint. For example, "Johnny bugs me, but he does help me with my homework."

A third strategy is to subtly keep a list of all the child's complaints during a day. Then present them in a straightforward manner: "Peter, here is your list of complaints for today. I notice that you had fifteen of them." When given that information, the child may see the need to deal with the behavior.

17. Handle Demanding Behavior

Some children find that incessant demanding satisfies their need for attention. Accordingly, ignore demanding behavior. When children learn to make requests in a polite manner, however, listen to them and treat them with respect. But don't inadvertently reward demanding behavior by giving in just to achieve peace.

18. Deal with Jealousy

Jealousy—including talking unkindly about others, complaining about being left out, or not having new things—may be another form of inappropriate attention-seeking behavior. To diffuse jealousy, point children toward activities that will help them grow in self-confidence, self-satisfaction, and self-worth. Encouragement and compliments may help deal with the feelings that trigger jealousy. Direct them toward peers who have similar ability levels, and who aren't jealous, and who don't complain or harp. Remind older children of the consequences of their jealous behavior, which can include losing friendships and alienating others.

19. Contend with the Crybaby

Some children can turn the tears on whenever they feel they need some added attention. Rewarding more acceptable and appropriate means of expressing frustration and disappointment should help decrease whimpering. Ignoring the tears and removing the audience also may be helpful. Make sure that other children or adults don't inadvertently reward bawling. Dealing with the problem in a calm way reinforces the message that "crying doesn't pay."

20. Deal with a Bragger

In our competitive culture, children, like adults, tend to pursue one-up-manship. Parents can help point out the consequences of bragging—loss of friendships and the respect of others. Children can increase their self-confidence and self-worth by participating in activities where they can experience reasonable success. Love and respect are not based on having more possessions than others or beating them in sports.

Peer Relationship Problems

Home is where parents have the strongest basis for power and control regarding their children's behavior, including consequences, rewards, and negative repercussions. At school, the authoritative power is relegated to teachers. In the neighborhood, when youngsters are playing together, there may be no adult in command. It's in the neighborhood that they first begin to develop social skills without parental feedback. This can lead to peer relationship problems.

Parents can take a number of steps in dealing with these problems.

1. Tame the Bully

It seems every neighborhood has obnoxious children who want to throw their weight around. Bullies are not just boys. Girls also assume that role.

Instead of forbidding your child to play with the bully, invite the bully to your house. That way, you have the chance to exercise some control over the interactions. The impact of this strategy can be increased if other well-behaved youngsters are also invited. In the context of a group of appropriately mannered children, the bully will often show compliance, especially if the parents in that atmosphere display love and caring.

2. Ignore the Rough Edges

When children are in grade school, they often go through a period of using coarse language and poor manners as a way of showing independence and signaling their identification with a peer group. For the most part, you will be happiest and most comfortable if you ignore these temporary disruptions. If children are brought up in a caring atmosphere with high standards and get along well with their siblings, they'll adjust happily to other children and will subsequently become contented adults.

Middle childhood is often a time for the formation of secret clubs and groups. These dynamics involve conflict between "insiders" and "outsiders." Parents may become upset if they feel their child has become an elitist or chauvinist by not allowing certain youngsters into the group, conversely if their child is considered an outsider and not accepted by the "in group." With guidance, children usually can work through these phases quite well without lasting detrimental effects.

3. Evaluate Popularity

In junior and senior high school, adolescents value popularity. Sometimes they exaggerate its importance, believing that if they're not in the popular group, they're failures and will always be failures. And parents are usually happy when their children are considered popular and chagrined when they aren't.

Don't push popularity on your teens. If a child is naturally popular because of good social skills, athletic talent, or leadership abilities, that popularity should be accepted and enjoyed. But if children aren't popular, don't force them to pay a price for it. To do so could result in a child giving in to peer demands that promote unacceptable behavior. Without realizing it, parents can indirectly force their children into alcohol or drug abuse, cigarette smoking, or early sexual activity.

4. Expect Peer Pressure

By junior high, children find that to be accepted by their peers they must wear their hair a certain way, don fashionable clothes or shoes, or put on a particular type of makeup. Dealing with this issue requires common sense. It doesn't seem in children's best interests to force them to conform to a particular style of attire just because it's chic. But children shouldn't dress so clearly outdated as to be objects of ridicule. Within reason, children should be allowed to have some say in their appearance.

5. Be a Good Model

Children will learn to resist the pressures of their peer group if they witness similar traits in their parents. If parents insist on driving a popular new car, having the trendiest house or clothing, and going to the right parties given by the right people, their children soon learn that popularity and acceptance are important values. But if the parents follow their own standards, children will conclude that integrity, independence, and self-assurance are more important than popularity.

6. Help the Shy Child

Children who are forced to stay away from their neighborhood companions may become withdrawn and isolated. Don't prevent a child from associating with peers who may appear to be undesirable. The goal instead should be to control the child's interactions more carefully.

One way to help the shy child is to talk with a teacher about setting up some kind of positive experience. Nothing combats low self-esteem better than success in the classroom, as well as at home or play.

Parents can help by encouraging their child to invite a playmate to go along on an outing, such as a picnic or camping trip. Organized parents can engineer such social events so that they become pleasant experiences for the children involved.

Some children are slow developers, and they should not be pushed into every social situation. It would be a mistake, for example, to force a slow-developing male to begin dating before he's ready.

Although it's generally a good idea to provide early social experiences for children, these interactions need to be supervised. Unsupervised early events can result in discomfort if children are teased, embarrassed, or ridiculed.

Role-playing with family members can also help develop positive interaction skills, and movies and other filmed activities can provide examples and models.

You can also help an isolated child become more involved with peers by asking a popular child to accompany them on a special trip or by encouraging the child to join clubs and other activities.

Reward and encourage your child even for small improvements. Some shy children feel more comfortable with younger children. Thus, they can acquire better social skills by taking care of younger children, with appropriate supervision. They may need to be taught how to ask basic conversational and open-ended questions, and also may benefit from learning how to shake hands, stand assertively, and project inner confidence in general.

Shy children also may find it helpful when their parents interact assertively and comfortably, and don't show shyness during their own personal encounters.

7. Think Straight

Frequently, the problem with peer relationships lies more in the parents' mind than anywhere else. Parents often invest so much in their child that they tie their own value to their youngster's popularity and begin to think irrationally. They conjure up the notion that if their child isn't popular, they're failures as parents. Such attitudes only reinforce the child's dependence on peer pressure.

Although peer popularity is an important ingredient in self-esteem, it's not the only one. Many children who are respected, but not necessarily included in the most popular groups, have no problems with self-esteem.

8. Deal with Undesirable Companions

Some adolescents insist on hanging out with groups that engage in borderline predelinquent activities. The more parents try to discourage children from associating with undesirable companions, the more likely they are to sneak out and do it anyway, which can lead to a deteriorating parent-child relationship. In such cases, the child can earn the opportunity to associate with these friends by responsible behavior. Tell your child that associating with these friends is a privilege that must be earned. To earn this privilege, he needs to demonstrate self-control and responsibility in other areas—for example, grades, a part-time job, or tasks around the house. By improving responsibility and self-control in these areas, he will be less likely to fall under the influence of a negative peer group.

With some adolescents, a mutual problem-solving strategy may work. Parents might casually observe that when children are with certain friends, they get into difficulty. In this case, a parent might say, "Jan, whenever you're playing with Patricia after school, you seem to get into trouble by not following the rules we set at home. How do you propose to deal with this problem?" Don't forbid a relationship with an undesirable companion. Instead, let children come to the realization that such relationships are unhealthy.

9. Use Logical Challenge and Disputation

Use logic and reasoning with adolescents. In a calm, nonthreatening way, explore the teenager's contradictory behavior with respect to peer pressure. Point out that it's important for the youth to be independent and that the pressure of the peer group is making that difficult or impossible.

Another strategy is to confront children with questions like, "What's going to happen if you don't do what your friends tell you to do?" Through persistent challenging, children eventually admit, if only to themselves, that nothing horrible will happen if they don't do what's "cool."

10. Talk It Over

With companionship problems, viable solutions can be obtained if the two sets of parents work out solutions to the problem. Often one set of parents may have only a partial grasp of the problem, whereas both sets can obtain a much better hold on it. Two sets of open-minded parents can cooperate and work together for the well-being of their children.

11. Expand the Circle of Friends

Sometimes an undesirable child in the neighborhood can have a negative influence on other youngsters even after various kinds of interventions. In this case, parents should try to expand their child's circle of friends without attempting to eliminate the undesirable companion.

12. Know the Value of Fear

In dealing with children who are associating with delinquent or predelinquent peers, try using a scare tactic. The movie *Scared Straight* is often shown in adolescent groups to sensitize them to the possible consequences of criminal behavior. (This movie can be rented from your local video store or purchased from Pyramid Film and Video, Box 1048, Santa Monica, CA 90406.)

In many areas of the country, there are correctional facilities—often called "ranches" or "farms"—for delinquent boys that are highly structured and use a positive peer program. The staff at these institutions may offer special weekend experiences for predelinquent boys to acquaint them with the potential consequences of their behavior.

Although this scare tactic doesn't work in all cases, it has been successful at least 25 percent of the time in our experience. Another approach is to ask a police officer or probation officer to talk to youth and perhaps take them to jail to show the possible consequences of delinquency.

13. Get Tough

In both junior and senior high school, many students are subjected to harassment and extortion. They're told that if they don't pay a certain protection fee or join a particular gang, they'll be beaten up. In these extreme situations, a clearly assertive stance is indicated.

Contact the police and report the criminal behavior. Or call a lawyer who could contact the offenders' parents, threatening them with a charge of contributing to the delinquency of a minor.

14. Tell It Like It Is

Sexual activity is an area that's especially vulnerable to peer pressure. This is particularly true for girls who feel that their popularity among boys will be enhanced if they engage in sexual intercourse.

The best way to deal with this kind of sexual attitude is prevention. Adolescents need to be well informed about the consequences of sexual behavior, including pregnancies, diseases, and marred reputations. More important, they need to learn assertive strategies for saying no without feeling guilty or fearing rejection. They need to learn responses such as, "Thanks for the compliment, but I'm not interested right now."

If sexual intercourse does occur, whether or not it results in pregnancy, parents frequently overreact. It's better to deal with this problem in a calm, rational way.

In the event of unplanned pregnancy, it's best for the adolescent, in most cases, not to raise a child. If the parent and/or child is uncomfortable about abortion, then adoption should be encouraged. The probability of an adolescent mother abusing a child is exceedingly high.

15. Accept Friendships

Often children seem to have a "best friend." Sometimes they appear to associate exclusively with that companion, spending hours on the phone or in play. Although this may become an area of concern, don't interfere. To do so is to invite rebellion. Exclusive friendships aren't necessarily damaging. From such associations, children can learn a great deal about meaningful interpersonal relationships that can help them to mature.

16. Exert Subtle Influence

Although we want our children to choose their own friends, there may be times when it's beneficial for some friendships to be encouraged more than others. Children learn to be like their peers. They pick up the mannerisms and interpersonal styles of those with whom they associate.

In many instances, children mature nicely by associating with those peers who have complementary personalities. For example, parents can subtly encourage a shy child to have more outgoing companions. A dependent, clinging, whining child may benefit from association with more independent companions.

17. Have Expectations

The expectations that parents communicate to their youngsters are powerful behavioral influences. If parents express confidence in their children's decision-making abilities, and trust them to stay out of trouble with friends, they're likely to comply.

18. Avoid Jealousy

Most parents aren't willing to admit to being jealous of their child's other relationships. But it does occur. When a child begins to move away from the family and establish peer associations, parents often become envious. This jealousy can be especially pronounced when heterosexual relationships are involved. For example, fathers can become quite jealous of their daughters' boyfriends.

It may hurt parents when their children confide in others, but they need to admit that it is their problem and they need to accept it.

19. Practice Role-Playing

Children often encounter socialization problems they aren't equipped to handle, such as teasing or insults. It can be helpful to work through these situations with role-playing.

To do this, children first explain what happened. Then they describe how it was handled and how they would like to have handled it. Next assume the roles, with the parents playing the children and the children acting as the aggressors. In this way, parents can model some appropriate responses. Then reverse the roles so that children can try out a new skill.

20. Stay Informed

Children's and teenager's worlds are constantly changing. Parents need to stay informed about those worlds. They can't assume that because some expressions remain the same, the experiences will not change. For example, "going steady" is a popular term. But it means something different now than it did in the 1950s and 1960s.

21. Tolerate Fads

Adolescents don't become enamored of radical thinkers and bizarre movements by chance. It's part of their search for meaning and identity. Characteristically, today's teens are plagued with self-doubt, discouragement, and fear of failure. In desperation, and often without much rationale, they look to the philosophies of rebellion and radicalism. They lack the courage and insight to work out their own solutions to these perpetual problems, so they jump on the bandwagon of a movement.

Just as it's important not to criticize your child's choice of friends, it's also not a good idea to disparage fads. Children are likely to perceive criticism as a lack of understanding and support. Furthermore, criticism of this nature further widens the chasm of communication between parents and adolescents.

22. Downplay Competition

An irrational emphasis on competition in our culture has become a bedrock for destructive peer pressure. We've become subtly brainwashed into believing that we have to be the biggest and best at everything.

Parents can effectively guide their child's view of competition if they view it as an intrapersonal, rather than interpersonal, phenomenon. In other words, competition, for the most part, shouldn't involve other people.

Standards, goals, aspirations, and wishes should be one's own, and not seen as competing with others. People should set their own pace, not let it be dictated by others.

23. Plan Your Attack

A dilemma occurs for many parents when they find out about antisocial or predelinquent behavior among their children's friends. They don't know whether to contact that child's parents and convey their knowledge.

For example, a child runs away from home and goes to a friend's home to seek protection. If the friend's parents don't level with the child's parents and report the incident, they may be contributing to the delinquency of a minor. If they do report the incident, they may violate the relationship between their child and the runaway companion.

In general, it's not desirable to protect delinquent children unless there are indications that not doing so will lead to some extremely adverse circumstances. For example, if the child in question is the victim of parental abuse, it may not be in the youngster's best interest to be sent back home. It may be better to call authorities.

24. Use Empathy

It's important to be supportive and to communicate understanding regarding peer relationship problems. Children often use the expression, "Everybody else is doing it." When that occurs, state sympathetically that you realize it's difficult to go against the grain of the group. But gently make it clear that conformity is not desirable in all cases. Conformity is one choice, but not the only one.

25. Take the Blame

Sometimes adolescents need an acceptable reason or excuse to give to their peers when they do not want to engage in the behavior of their peer group. In this case, let the adolescents know they can always use you as the reason for not engaging in an undesirable behavior. For example, if a peer group is interested in drinking alcohol and the adolescent doesn't really want to do that, he or she can say to the group, "I can't go with you. My parents will kill me if I come home and they smell alcohol on my breath. I don't want to risk not being able to go out with you guys ever again. My parents are really strict about this so I'm not going to go with you." A peer group is more likely to accept having unreasonable and uncool parents as opposed to simply not wanting to engage in the behavior. Most parents are willing to be used as an excuse and take the blame when their adolescent does not want to engage in an undesirable and unsafe behavior with their peer group.

Aggression and Fighting

Aggression can be defined as an action with intent to hurt another person through physical or verbal means. It's one of parents' major complaints about their children and is often accompanied by other problems.

Aggression may involve assault and physical attacks or threats, teasing, sarcasm, and provocation. In general, aggressive children are excitable, impulsive, immature, and reckless. They often have interpersonal problems because they're unpopular and on the fringes of their peer group. Aggression in young children is a correlate of the same trait in adults. In other words, aggressive children often become aggressive adults. Aggression is most prevalent among preschoolers. If it persists into middle childhood, it should be considered a serious problem.

Here are a few suggestions for controlling aggressive childhood behavior.

1. Take Steps Early to Prevent Aggression

Because aggression often leads to chronic relationship and self-esteem problems, steps need to be taken early to prevent it. Children who have warm parents and are in a consistent disciplinary atmosphere have the lowest probability of aggressiveness. Indulgent, lax, overly permissive, and hostile parents tend to raise highly aggressive children. Inconsistency and laxity coupled with hostility convey the attitude the parent doesn't really care.

Carefully monitoring a child's exposure to filmed violence can reduce a tendency toward aggression. Similarly, if a child is exposed to a conflict-oriented, argumentative, and hostile atmosphere, the probability of aggressive impulsivity is higher. Also, because of the natural aggressive tendencies of preschoolers, it's important to have adequate supervision when children of that age play together.

2. Ignore Aggression

Many children are aggressive because they want attention, and one sure way to get it is to hit others. In these cases, systematically ignoring aggression can be helpful in the long run. Ignoring behavior is a calculated action. Give no attention to the aggressive child. There should be no eye contact or verbal exchange.

3. Reward Cooperation

Combine ignoring aggressive behavior with a reward program. If you reward a desired behavior and ignore the opposite, positive change will occur. When a child cooperates nicely with a friend, express praise and perhaps even give a tangible reward.

Another strategy for reducing aggression is to reward children for the time when such activity is absent. For example, set up a charting system. Every time a child goes an hour without the specified aggressive behavior, give him a check or star that could later be exchanged for a reward. If aggression does occur during that hour, then nothing goes on the chart. Naturally, supplement the star or check with verbal praise.

4. Improve Verbal Skills

Many aggressive children are also inarticulate. They have difficulty expressing themselves clearly and intelligently. Helping them improve their verbal skills can reduce aggressive tendencies. For instance, instead of hitting someone who takes something away from them, the child could learn to say, "You took the truck I was playing with. That makes me very upset. Please give it back."

5. Find Alternatives

In their book *Problem Solving Techniques in Child Rearing,* Drs. Myrna Shure and George Spivack have described a strategy to help preschoolers increase their social judgment ([San Francisco: Jossey-Bass, 1978], chap. 2). The child is required to think of all kinds of possible solutions to a specific problem. For example, the parent might say, "Jason took your truck away. What could you do or say to get it back?" As the child describes a possible course of action, the parent then states, "That's one thing you could do. What's another one?" The parent continues to ask for suggestions and to write them down on a piece of paper.

In the next stage, the parent helps the child anticipate the consequences of each possible solution. For example, if one suggested solution was to hit or fight with the other child, then some possible consequences might be physical or emotional pain, the anger of supervising adults, the loss of a friendship, or earning a bad reputation. Finally, after the child has listed consequences of the various solutions, he or she goes back over the list to determine the relative merits of each one.

Children don't learn this problem-solving strategy overnight. It takes countless repetitions. Nevertheless, it is an excellent model for dealing with the problem at hand and for handling other troubles that may arise.

6. Keep Your Perspective

Parents often become upset when their child displays aggression. Some imagine they will be looked down on by other parents for being ineffective and weak. Others catastrophize, imagining that the behavior pattern will continue until their child lands in prison.

Keep a child's aggressive behavior in perspective. Think to yourself: "I certainly don't approve of this behavior, but nothing horrible is going to happen because of it." Or "If neighbors think I'm an ineffective parent, I can live with that, although I don't like it. I truly do not need their approval of every one of my child's actions. I know that I'm doing what I can to eliminate aggressiveness."

7. Improve the Quality of the Child's Self-Talk

Many aggressive children are impulsive and reckless and lack self-control. Often their impulsivity can be controlled by improving the quality of their self-talk. Children can be taught to consistently say to themselves, "Stop, breathe, and think." Aggressive children need to be constantly reminded that alternative behavior can be acquired.

8. Limit Aggressive Models

It's important to control a child's exposure to filmed violence. In addition, monitor your own behavior and that of your acquaintances in the company of your children. If parents or their friends tend to be quick-tempered, verbally abrasive, sarcastic, critical, loud, or argumentative, those traits are likely to be acquired by their children.

Parents who don't wish to deprive their children of TV programs should monitor filmed violence. The adult is there to remind children that what they're seeing is make-believe, and to point out the potential dangers of violence.

9. Release Anger

Children can be taught that although it's inappropriate to express angry impulses toward people, they can show their rage by hitting a doll, a pillow, or a punching bag. They can be allowed to draw or paint pictures to release their anger. The opportunity to release aggressive feelings through participation in organized sports also is desirable. Like adults, some children can effectively dissipate their anger through aerobic exercises such as biking, running, and swimming.

10. Use Negative Consequences

Isolation is often good discipline for aggressive behavior. As previously discussed, a child should be put into a boring area for approximately one minute per year of age. Another possibility is removing privileges. Or the aggressor can apologize and make restitution by doing a favor for the victim.

11. Try Creative Distractions

Once in a while, it's possible to use aggressive conflict as an opportunity for creative diversion. If two children are fighting with each other and knock over a chair, you might say, "Bob and Jim, when you knocked that chair over, I just realized something important. We forgot to rearrange your bedroom as we promised. Let's do it right now. Let's move the bed first." In a calm, collected manner, focus on a minor aspect of the conflict but translate it into something else.

12. Provide a Time and Place

Children, like adults, need to know that expressing anger is healthy, as long as it's done at an appropriate time and place. Children need an outlet for their rage, and you must identify the situation in which it's acceptable to show anger. When a child is calm, say, "Mary, from now on, when you start to feel really mad and destructive, I won't say anything, but I'll give you a signal by touching my nose. When I do that, you can decide to either stop expressing your anger or go to your room and hit your pillow."

13. Allow Symbolic Expression

Children can constructively vent their anger if given an opportunity to express it creatively and symbolically. For instance, ask older children to write a letter to a favorite person, explaining why they're upset. Younger children could draw a picture portraying their feelings and send it to a favorite person.

14. Engage in Role-Playing

In role-playing situations, children re-enact recent conflicts. In this way, they can look at their own behavior and learn how to better control it. If two children are fighting over a game, for example, they might be asked to go through the episode again after their tempers have cooled, using their exact words and actions. Then they might be asked to change roles, all the while trying to come up with a better solution.

15. Learn Other Behaviors

For chronically aggressive children, stress behaviors that are incompatible with fighting. In practice sessions, the child can learn different behaviors. Have children role-play those situations that typically spur belligerence, and learn to pursue a behavior that's incompatible with it. For example, they might get a drink of water, leave the situation, or pick up a book and start reading. The goal is clear. As soon as children feel the urge to be aggressive, they turn away and engage in another behavior, thereby replacing one habit with another.

16. Use Protective Gear

For aggressive and fighting behavior, have a set of protective gear available for both children. This gear can consist of helmets, shoulder pads, a shield of sorts, knee pads, and other kinds of equipment that protect a person from physical injury. It should not consist of any kind of weaponry or objects that can be used in retaliation. When a fight is ensuing or behavior is mounting to a more aggressive level, intervene by making a production of the issue: Say, "Wait, wait. You have to get dressed for this." Then get out the protective gear and have the children put it on. Keep adding layers and layers of protective gear until the anger is diffused. This kind of interruption can be just enough to reduce the aggressive behavior of the children so that a more reasonable and calm solution can be discussed.

Chapter Three

Minding and Cooperation

Compliance in General

In every family, children should obey promptly without dawdling and defiance. In stressful and dangerous situations, a child needs to follow parents' directions for everyone's well-being. The goal isn't to make children respond like robots. But a parent must establish strategies, so that children follow directions promptly.

Any time one family member shirks responsibilities, it puts an unfair burden on the others. In a family, everyone must work together. It's up to parents to teach their children to cooperate. Some do it by threats and spankings. Some scream and nag. Some just give up and let the child rule.

Despite changing attitudes toward violent parenting, many adults still spank non-compliant children. We firmly believe that spanking isn't a beneficial form of discipline for children. Some parents and educators believe that a few swift cracks on a child's buttocks punish misbehavior without lasting emotional harm. But that approach can become a habit. It also teaches children violence. And severe physical and emotional injury can occur when beatings persist. We also oppose verbal and emotional abuse, such as screaming and nagging. Any way you look at it, both parents and children will be better off if more peaceful forms of discipline are used.

Children characteristically grumble, complain, and dawdle. But they'll usually follow instructions if they're given an opportunity to vent their dislikes. They don't have to like what they're told to do. That's their right. Similarly, parents don't have to give a rationale for their rules. But explaining that rationale may be helpful in obtaining compliance.

There are many possible strategies that can help parents teach their children compliance.

1. Give Fewer Orders

If orders, as opposed to requests, are the usual fare, then children are less likely to comply. Demands should be made infrequently. With younger children especially, establish an environment that requires few orders. Child-proofing the environment can reduce the need to give orders.

But parental commands must result in compliance. When you give orders, you must be ready to follow through. For that reason, distinguish between making requests and giving orders. A request allows children a choice. But an order requires that children comply. If they refuse, you must impose consequences.

In giving instructions to children, many parents offer multiple-step directions. This can lead to confusion and inaction, which parents interpret as deliberate noncompliance. Instead, give one- or two-step directions. Some older children can handle three-step directions.

2. Let the Child Know

Work out consequences jointly to be used when a child refuses to obey an order, then share that information with the child. Explain what will happen if directions aren't followed.

3. Use Isolation

We agree with behaviorists who suggest isolation for children who don't obey. Find the most boring place to use for a time-out. A quiet corner in the dining room or a long hallway may be appropriate. A stairwell might work, or the parents' bedroom.

In using this technique, tell children that if they don't follow the order by the count of three, the consequence will be isolation. Isolation should last a minimum of one minute for every year of age. A child who leaves the isolation area before time is up is to be put back firmly and silently. Use a timer if necessary to measure the time period. The child shouldn't stay in isolation longer than the designated time. When the time is up, give the order again. If compliance doesn't occur by the count to three, repeat the isolation.

As the child finishes the second isolation and comes out again, repeat the order. If there's still no compliance, begin the cycle again. Don't give up on this strategy once it has been initiated, and don't give orders unless you're prepared to follow through for as long as necessary.

4. Try the Exit Program

Some psychologists suggest a different approach to the problem of noncompliance. They believe children disobey their parents because they love the attention their noncompliance brings. One way to eliminate that attention is by separating from the child after giving directions. For example, retire to the bedroom or bathroom. Or leave the house, provided this situation doesn't endanger young children. When you return, repeat the request. If the child still won't comply, leave again.

5. Keep Cool

In helping children become compliant at home, stay calm and cool. When parents lose control, they punish excessively and later regret it. Then they may be tempted to undo the punishment. When that happens, children learn all the wrong things. They assume the unpleasantness they experienced was due to parental anger and not to their own misbehavior, and that their parents won't follow through with discipline.

6. Use the Evil Eye

Dr. Dan Kiley suggests another approach for dealing with mild noncompliance in younger children (*Keeping Kids out of Trouble* [New York: Warner Books, 1978], 144–145). When children don't follow directions, Kiley recommends the parent stare at them without saying a word or changing facial expression. It may be necessary to hold their shoulders so they're fully aware of getting the evil eye. Then the parent should repeat the order in a firm tone of voice.

7. Try Deprivation

With older children, especially adolescents, isolation in their rooms may not be effective for noncompliance. Social isolation may be more beneficial. Children can be grounded to the yard, deprived of phone privileges, or made to come home and stay home after school. Other penalties could include losing use of a bike or car. The object is to deprive the child of something important to him or her, but for only a limited period of time.

8. Use Empathic Reinforcement

If children don't want to mind, first recognize the children's wish. For example, if the child is playing and you want her to put her toys away, you could say, "You'd like to continue playing with your toys because you're really having a good time." The next step would be for the parent to underline and clarify the rules of the house. "The rule is, no playing after 8:00." Then help her identify another way to at least partially fulfill her desire, if not now, then at a later date. "You can play with your toys tomorrow morning or tomorrow afternoon." The last step is to help the child get in touch with feelings of anger and resentment because rules and restrictions have been imposed. For example, "I know that you don't like that rule. I know you wish that rule didn't exist." Only if the children don't follow through is any kind of gentle physical restraint put into action.

9. Use Positive Feedback

Encourage compliant and conforming behavior with positive consequences. When children follow directions, thank them and treat them like human beings. Some physical attention like a smile, a hug, mussing up of their hair, or a squeeze of the shoulder can be very positive. It's not important to do this every single time that compliance occurs. But it's quite apparent that children need attention; if they don't get it for positive behavior, they'll seek it through negative actions.

10. Implement the Point System

A reward program can help enhance cooperative behavior. This can be created by charting daily responsibilities and requests. Responsibilities are usually fixed from day to day. But depending on a number of variables, the spontaneous requests and directions may vary considerably.

Use a formal charting system with directions written on the chart and with boxes for each day of the week so that the appropriate mark can be made if compliant behavior occurs. In using a point system, be consistent and reliable. Supplement tangible rewards with verbal praise and hugs.

A reward system is most effective when combined with a negative-consequence system for failure to do the work. In other words, if the child does what's requested, give a reward; if the child refuses, use a negative consequence. In either case, there's a consequence. The consistent application of the two types of consequences usually results in a significant decrease in noncompliance.

11. Make a Contract

With older children, especially adolescents, create a written contract. This arrangement would indicate particular behaviors that the child agrees to perform and the reciprocal action that you will take if the child complies. The agreement needs to be specific, with definite time limits. It should be signed by the parent, the child, and a witness. Each contract should contain a clause allowing for mutual renegotiation if necessary.

12. Win the War, but Not Every Battle

It's impossible to fight a full-blown war on every battlefront. As children get older, the possibilities for disagreement increase. Hairstyle, clothing, and companions can become sources of contention. Show a willingness to cooperate. Don't insist on absolute compliance in every area, especially those of lesser importance.

13. Use the Silent Treatment

In cases of severe noncompliance, use the silent treatment to achieve cooperation. This method requires your commitment to follow through until cooperation is obtained. With this approach, you totally ignore the child. He is not spoken to or looked at. No one plays with him. No meals are set out for children who can fix their own. The only mention of his name comes in casual conversation with others. If someone asks about him, you might say, "Pete can play after he takes out the trash." Usually, it takes a while for children to comprehend the nature of this strategy. When they finally understand what's going on, they may become furious and throw a temper tantrum. If so, simply wait it out.

Some children may resist for hours, even days. However, if all members of the family work together, the child will begin to realize that the consequences of noncompliance aren't worth the struggle. If noncompliance is repeated, repeat the same strategy until it works. This isn't a strategy we recommend for the garden variety of noncooperation. But in cases of persistent misbehavior, it's an option to consider.

14. Establish Self-Control

A restraining strategy can be used with extremely obstinate, defiant children. It's to be used only when children resist all adult authority and are totally out of control, endangering themselves and others. There are two major components in this strategy. First, hold or restrain the child so she cannot move. The restraining position can vary with the size of the child. Younger children, for instance, can sit on your lap while you keep one leg draped over the child for restraint. Then hold the child's torso and grasp her hands. It should be done gently without hurting the child.

With older children, kneel on the floor and straddle the child's back, using your knees to confine the youngster, and your hands to firmly press the child's shoulders to the floor. If the child is particularly strong, this method may require two or more adults. It should be done gently without hurting the child.

When the child is safely restrained, state, "I'm going to hold you like this until you can control yourself." When the child appears to be calmer, the parent can let him go. This solution should rarely, if ever, be used.

15. Try a Paradoxical Approach

Sometimes in mild cases of noncompliance, it's possible to gain control over an insubordinate child by doing something totally out of character. For example, when a child is misbehaving, a parent might smilingly hand her a piece of fruit, saying, "Here, have an apple." Or the parent might compliment her for something that's irrelevant at the time. For instance, "Sally, I was very proud of the fact that you acted so politely at the family reunion." Paradoxical strategies such as these often catch children off guard and may quell a noncompliant mood.

16. Make Sure It's Heard

Children are much more likely to follow directions if they can repeat them. There's a greater likelihood of the child repeating directions if there haven't been any distractions, if he has made eye contact with the person giving the directions, and if the adult has maintained undivided attention.

17. Give a Forced Choice

In getting a child to be cooperative, give the appearance of her having a choice. This can be done by providing options that are acceptable to you both. The child must believe that she has control over the situation and can impact her future, while in actuality, you are providing a forced choice situation where she is cooperative. For example, "Do you want to clean your room now or at 3:00?"

When children learn to cooperate and listen to their parents' directions, the family can begin assigning household responsibilities in a fair manner.

Responsibility

The issue of responsibility is important to family and individual growth. For families to be happy and harmonious, there needs to be a fair distribution of labor. Beginning with preschoolers, all members of a family need to shoulder some share of household responsibility. In this section of our book, we discuss how parents can help children cooperate in carrying out regular responsible behaviors. For the most part, this means performing tasks on a routine basis that help the whole family. These would include feeding pets, vacuuming, cooking meals, doing dishes, buying groceries, taking out the garbage, and recycling.

1. Give an Allowance

Many disciplinarians are strongly opposed to any connection between allowances and chores. Behaviorists, however, believe that children should be rewarded, at least initially, for responsible behavior, including the completion of chores. Just as many adults don't work if they aren't paid, most children won't work unless there's a tangible reward for doing so. Also, while most behaviors aren't automatic, autonomous, or self-perpetuating at first, they may become so in time. For example, once a child is in the habit of feeding the dog, this behavior will go on even if the tangible rewards become less. Once children brush their teeth regularly, rewards can be phased out as the habit continues.

Some behaviorists argue that it's sometimes necessary to "prime

Chore Chart

Week of _____ Child _____

Chore	Sun	Mon	Tue	Wed	Thu	Fri	Sat
Make bed							
Do dinner dishes							
Feed and water pets							
Put dirty clothes in laundry basket							
Sweep kitchen floor							

the pump" to stimulate responsible actions. Allowances can do that. One effective method is the use of a "chore chart," which may be posted on the refrigerator. The chart shows the days of the week across the top and the chores in the left-hand column. Each time a chore is completed in an appropriate manner, a check is entered in the respective box. Each check is worth money. At the end of the week, the allowance is given. The use of a bonus is encouraged when a child has earned every single one of the checks.

2. Earn Privileges

An alternative to the allowance system is the privilege system. A similar chart can be used. Points can be earned for completing chores responsibly. The points work toward certain privileges. For example, it might cost 15 points to go to the shopping mall or 25 to go to a movie. The key is the privileges need to be earned through responsible behavior.

3. Allow Logical Consequences

A parent can work out an agreement beforehand, in which the children freely agree that the chores need to be done before they can go to bed. Once that agreement occurs, put it into action. If children go to bed without doing their chores, they can be awakened in the middle of the night, for instance, and reminded to do them at that time.

4. Go on Strike or Vacation

In situations where a number of children are not cooperating in carrying out their chores, a dramatic but effective strategy can be used. The parents, for example, simply buy groceries but do not prepare meals. They inform the children what is happening and eat elsewhere during the mealtime. In addition, no laundry, house cleaning, or other adult chores are done. In other words, the parents go on strike until the children's behavior improves.

For this technique to work, all other adults who have contact with the children must be informed and agree not to sabotage the program. The children are left to do their own cooking and take care of themselves. The parents simply provide supervision in a calm, matter-of-fact manner. This would only work with children who are old enough to take care of themselves.

This is a very complex approach that should be used only in severe cases of noncompliance. It may take as long as a week before the strategy even begins to take effect. Once the children have agreed to complete their chores, the parental strike should end, but with the clear understanding that it will resume if irresponsible childhood behavior begins again. The parental strike can also be used in a limited way if some specific acts of irresponsibility occur. For example, if the only major problem is getting children to do the dishes, then the parental strike could involve not fixing meals. If the area of concern is dirty clothes, then the parents simply refuse to do the laundry. Once again, it's important to use this strategy when parents are calm and collected.

5. Teach Through Modeling

Parents teach children responsibility not through their words, but through their behavior. If parents handle their chores responsibly, children are likely to do the same. Modeling also involves demonstrating how various chores are to be done. Children may benefit from watching parents take out the garbage efficiently. A wise parent demonstrates carefully how to change cat litter before assigning that chore to a child.

6. Don't Make Mountains out of Molehills

Learning responsibility is important as children develop. At certain stages, some irresponsibility is to be expected, however, and the emotional strain that parents direct toward altering nature's course hardly seems worth it. For example, many pre-adolescents (around ages ten, eleven, and twelve) seem to be reluctant to become involved in taking care of their possessions or their hygiene. As a result, their bedrooms resemble a junkyard. In the long run, it may be easier for parents simply to insist that the door to the room remain closed, rather than constantly harping on the need for clean-up.

7. Give a Voice, but Not a Choice

Simple compliance is not the equivalent of responsibility. Although children may go through the motions of completing chores, including making their beds or washing dishes, such overt responsibility in and of itself may not positively influence the development of self-discipline. Merely keeping one's room neat and doing assigned chores doesn't assure responsible decisions in other areas. Responsibility is not innate, nor is it automatically acquired at the age of reason. Like any other skill, it's acquired slowly over long years of practice. Children can exercise choices about responsibilities that are age-appropriate. With those that fall within the parental realms, the child may have a voice, but not a choice.

8. Assign Age-Appropriate Chores

When a child requests a particular privilege, parents often give in after a certain amount of nagging, feeling that they've somehow come out the victor because they've demanded that the child take on responsibility for a new privilege. One example might be buying a pet. Children may nag and pester their parents to purchase a pet. The parents finally give in, but insist that the child has to take responsibility for feeding, grooming, and cleaning the pet. Unless the child is at least in middle adolescence, this level of responsible behavior will not occur; many frustrations, threats, and conflicts may result. Keep the child's developmental level in perspective when assigning responsibilities.

9. Keep Chores in Perspective

If irresponsibility with respect to chores and duties becomes a major scene of turmoil and explosiveness in a family, parents should evaluate their underlying principles and assumptions about those chores. Oftentimes, parents think that other adults will judge them harshly because their children don't exercise responsibility around the house. Some parents believe that because their children don't easily and cooperatively assume household duties, they'll become failures as adults. If parents can keep their own heads clear and not be ruled by these irrational, self-defeating thoughts, they'll be better able to view and discuss the issue of chores in a matter-of-fact manner, and with better results.

10. Allow Failure

Oftentimes, children will complete a task or chore in a way that doesn't come up to the standards of the parent. When teaching responsibility, make sure children are reinforced for following through with the task. But if the task is not done perfectly, the child needs to be allowed to fail and perhaps try again. What is important is that they are doing the task—not that it is done in a perfect way.

Neatness

Many families struggle to achieve a happy medium between compulsive perfectionism and slovenly chaos. Both extremes can leave most people frustrated. Children who are excessively or compulsively neat and clean are usually rigid, fearful, and highly dependent. On the other hand, children who are habitually sloppy also may have problems adjusting to society. The best alternative is a compromise.

A number of ideas can help parents achieve a realistic degree of neatness in the home.

1. Set an Example

Parents set the example. Neat parents tend to have neat children. Sloppy parents have sloppy children.

2. Give Rewards and Punishments

Chore charts can encourage children to show responsible behavior. Actions that could be specified on such a chart include cleaning up bedrooms, bathrooms, living rooms, basements, and playrooms. Appropriate follow-through with the behavior results in rewards, while not following through can mean a fine or loss of privilege.

3. Have Family Meetings

Family meetings are recommended for all families to discuss a variety of issues. Since neatness and cleanliness are issues that involve all members of the family, it's advisable to call everyone together and discuss concerns in an open, democratic manner. Using the principles of an open-ended family meeting, elicit possible solutions from your children. In the context of the family meeting, everyone can suggest solutions, and the best ones can be implemented. Discuss specific actions and responsibilities in a way that each child can easily understand. Don't discuss rewards or consequences shouldn't be discussed in the initial family meetings. Wait until a lack of cooperation indicates that additional measures are needed.

4. Use Untimely Reminders

Some approaches to child discipline discourage punishment while recommending that children be reminded of their unsatisfactory behavior at times that aren't convenient for them. In setting up this procedure, children must first agree on it.

A particularly inconvenient time for the children might be while they're asleep or about to fall asleep. After the child is in bed, begin knocking on the door about every fifteen minutes with a reminder that a particular task hasn't been completed. Another option is just to knock, waking the child, but not say anything until the required deed is done. Another good time for reminders is when the child is playing with friends or while at school, if the teacher or principal agrees to cooperate.

5. Institute Grandma's Rule

Children can simply be told that it's important to clean things up and put them away before eating, and that from now on food will be served to them only after required tasks are completed. If they come to the table without first having finished the cleanup, do not allow them to eat. Tell them firmly, "First you clean up, then you eat."

6. Try a Group Action

Often only one child in a family is guilty of a particular infraction, but the parents don't know which one. When this occurs, treat all children alike. For example, wake them all up at night and tell them something needs to be put away. This way, you refuse to get involved in arguments about who's responsible for the dastardly deed. You simply choose to let the children work that out and, in the meantime, to hold them all accountable.

7. Go on Strike

We've discussed the parental strike in previous sections. Here's another opportunity for its use. In this situation, both parents agree to act just like the rest of the family in all areas of the house except their own bedroom. They agree to stop nagging and reminding. They take care of their own rooms but nothing else. This procedure may take a long time to work, and it may not be wise to have any guests over during that time.

8. Confiscate, "Recycling Fairy"

Tell your children that the next time something is left lying around or out of place, it'll be locked away for an unspecified period of time, usually one to seven days. Put all the items collected during a given day into a bag, with the dates of the confiscation and release written on the outside. Then lock the bag in a closet or the trunk of a car.

9. Prevent It

From an early age, children can be taught to keep a neat room and put their toys away. If children can acquire the habit of being organized and not having their rooms in absolute chaos, they'll probably carry that habit into adulthood.

Even preschool-age children should have regular chores.

Preschoolers can learn to put their dirty clothes in a hamper or their toys in a certain place. As they reach the early grades, they can assume such responsibilities as vacuuming and making their beds. They also should be taught to become aware of their appearance—to comb their hair, tuck their shirts in, change into clean clothes, and wear reasonably coordinated clothing. They can also be involved in purchasing a toothbrush or hairbrush.

10. Have Patience

In helping children acquire the habit of neatness, it's important to reward small improvements. By their nature, children aren't perfectly clean and neat. Every tiny step they make toward improvement should be praised.

11. Give Responsibility and Privileges

As children get older, they often complain they're not given enough privileges. This can present an opportunity to point out that responsibilities are related to privileges. If children show an increase in responsibility, then they merit an increase in privileges. Neatness is an important area of responsibility. A messy child could put more effort into having a neat room. In return, parents might allow the child more privileges. Similarly, add privileges for greater grooming concern and appropriate care of clothing.

12. Try Role Reversal

Urge the messy child to monitor the other children in the family for a specified time, periodically observing and noting in detail the neatness or messiness of these siblings. Afterward, ask the reporter to discuss the notes with you privately or at a family meeting. In these discussions, he points out the social and practical implications of his siblings' behavior. If the behavior has been careless, the child can suggest to his siblings that they should be neater or cleaner. The object of this approach is to have the messy child acquire some concerns about neatness.

13. Make an Exception

Like most adults, children like to have one messy area. It might be a drawer, a closet, or an entire room. Children need a place where they don't have to worry about strict order. It's important, however, to carefully delineate spatial parameters so the child knows where and when messiness is allowed.

14. Use Routines

Some children are neater when they realize that there's an established and specified time each day during which they take care of all their belongings and put everything in its proper place. Clean clothes are hung up, and dirty clothes are put in the hamper. Toys are put in their proper places. School items are put away. During this special time of the day, every item goes in its own place.

15. Increase Storage

Sometimes children need additional storage space for their items. If this is the case, create storage compartments under their beds or organizational structures in their closets to increase their storage and the opportunity to be neat and organized.

Taking Care of Bedrooms and Personal Property

Parents use a wide variety of strategies to encourage children to keep their rooms neat and clean. Some nag and criticize. Others lecture and preach. Some bribe or use allowances and privileges, punishments, and fines. Others may simply ignore the situation.

Problems relating to personal property maintenance arise in all families, and there are a number of ways to deal with them.

1. Ignore It

With this approach, parents agree between themselves that the children's rooms are their own responsibilities, and how they are kept is the youngsters' own business. The parents agree not to become angry or nag about bedrooms.

It's a good idea to obtain a mechanical door closer so that the room is out of sight all the time. The sooner the room gets dirty and messy, the sooner the strategy will work. Children often have friends over who'll comment negatively about the condition of the room, inspiring the culprit to clean it up.

Remember that you aren't an ineffective parent just because your children have messy rooms. No matter what anyone says, the condition of a child's room is a reflection of the child, but not necessarily of the parent.

2. Ignore It, with Modifications

The ignoring procedure for room cleanliness may take months or even years to work. For parents who can't wait that long, there are alternatives. For example, tell the child that the status of the room will be ignored every day of the week except one. On that day—for instance, Saturday—the room must meet approval. Forbid the child to go out to play until the room is satisfactorily cleaned. No such criteria exist for the other six days of the week.

3. Use Behavioral Consequences

Many strategies discussed in other sections of this book also can be used for keeping a room presentable. These include Grandma's Rule, modeling, use of a chore chart, and others.

4. Use Reminders

Use reminders at inconvenient times to help children care for personal property. If a child habitually leaves a bike in the driveway or a front yard, remind him to put it away. Obtain prior agreement from the children to do this, making it clear that the reminding will be done at the most inconvenient time possible for the youngster.

5. Confiscate

Just as confiscation was used to remove items that hadn't been properly put away, it can be used with objects that have been improperly used. For instance, if children borrow tools and don't use them properly, the tools can be put off limits for one to seven days. Similarly, if children misuse some of their own equipment, it can be confiscated for a similar period.

6. Allow Natural Consequences

When children are forgetful, careless, or wasteful in dealing with their possessions, they need to face the consequence of irresponsible behavior. Children who lose their tennis shoes may simply be told, "There aren't any extra shoes, and there isn't any extra money to buy an additional pair. I guess you'll just have to wear other shoes until you find them."

The use of natural consequences should be based on an appropriate understanding of the child's developmental level. A small child can't be expected to keep track of all personal belongings at preschool, or to be responsible enough to take a valuable coin collection to class.

7. Institute Limits

For messy children, parents should limit the number of toys, clothes, or books that they're allowed to have in their room. There won't be any new toys or games until the old ones have been properly and responsibly taken care of.

8. Donate

A variation of the strategy of confiscation is to donate the items your children are unable to take care of or store properly. This strategy needs to be explained to children in advance, and you must follow through with donating the item to the charity or family that has been designated, even when children throw a fit in an attempt to win it back.

Chapter Four

Bad Habits

As children grow older, they often acquire bad habits. Some bite and chew their fingernails or toenails, or suck on their clothing; others scratch their genitals or pick their noses. Some continually curl their hair around their fingers and pluck it out.

Bad habits displayed at home or in public can embarrass parents. To discourage the bad habit, parents may reprimand their children. But for children who thrive on attention, this approach may encourage the behaviors. Parents who say, "Quit picking your nose," or give a child the evil eye or a sharp slap in order to curtail the habit, may make it worse.

Overcoming Bad Habits in General

Parents can help reduce bad habits, or eliminate them, by practicing one or more of the following suggestions.

1. Give Attention for Positive Behavior

Children have an almost insatiable need for attention. If they don't get enough attention for the positive things they do, they'll seek the negative kind, sometimes through bad habits. Instead of paying excessive attention to a child's irritating habit, be more attentive to other behaviors. Doing that successfully will usually prod bad habits to diminish.

Ignoring as a strategy takes a long time. Even if you never give in and refuse to reward a bad habit with attention, it can take at least a month before the behavior begins to change. The major problem with ignoring in this case is that one relapse on your part may wipe out all gains and make you go back to the beginning.

If you choose ignoring as a disciplinary tool, there are some things to keep in mind. If the child has several bad habits, it may not be wise to ignore all of them. This can prove much too difficult and stressful. Additionally, use both verbal and nonverbal ignoring. One way to do this without being overly dramatic or attention-getting is to look away, or walk away, but not in anger, because that conveys attention. Instead, act unconcerned about the behavior.

Children become frustrated when parents ignore them and may initially increase their misbehavior. At this point, some parents give up, assuming that ignoring doesn't work. But the fact that the child's behavior increases is actually proof that the strategy is working and should be continued. Eventually, the cycle of behavior will reserve itself.

Some habits aren't particularly offensive to parents, and can be ignored quite easily. These include sucking on clothes, nail biting, or hair twirling. Unless the child is mentally or emotionally disturbed, ignoring usually works over time. Other habits, such as playing with genitals or head-banging, aggravate parents, and can injure the child. These habits can't be ignored. Head-banging, in particular, demands that parents prevent youngsters from injuring themselves.

2. Allow Natural Consequences

Another strategy that can be used to change bad habits is the application of natural or logical consequences. For example, nose picking is unsanitary. As a result, it's not healthy to touch a nose picker or to eat at the same table with one. The same is true with nail biters or thumb suckers. Children displaying these habits can be required to eat alone.

As a preventive measure, children who twist their hair may have to have a portion of their hair cut off. Nail biters could have their nails trimmed. Children who constantly fondle their genitals can be required to take extra baths each day for hygienic reasons. In using these and other methods, parents should talk with the child beforehand in a calm, matter-of-fact way that doesn't convey anger, rejection, or punishment.

3. Be Realistic

Because bad childhood habits are embarrassing for parents, they can trigger negative, upsetting thoughts. For example, parents might think, "It would be awful if my parents found out that my child is a nose picker."

More realistic and healthy attitudes are essential if the parent is going to successfully deal with the problem. Replace overreactive thoughts with more rational ones, such as, "There's nothing really wrong with nose picking. I don't like it, but that doesn't mean it's the worst thing in the world. I wish my child wouldn't pick her nose, but if I handle it better and pay less attention, it will improve."

4. Be a Good Model

Whether they like to admit it or not, many parents have had bad habits. Children are keen observers, and mimic behavior of their parents. They hold their hands and cock their heads like their parents do. Parents who pick their nose often have nose-picking children. The moral is simple: One way to prevent bad habits in children is for parents to eliminate those habits themselves.

5. Respond to Danger Signals

When a dentist expresses concern about dental deformities because of thumb sucking, it's time to step in to change the habit. In general, when habits become dangerous, outside consultation is advised.

5. Enforce Practice Ad Nauseam

Another strategy is to have children practice their habits ad nauseam. With head bangers, for example, parents could place helmets on the children's heads and tell them to bang away. Parents need to supervise, however. When children get tired and want to quit, parents should insist they continue. With nose picking, parents could tell the child to keep picking and picking, even though there is no nasal mucus. The key is to make the child consciously practice the habit long enough to tire of it and want to quit.

Thumb Sucking

Some children continue sucking their thumbs past infancy. When children over the age seven or eight continue this habit, intervention is recommended.

1. Use Preventive Strategies

A number of early preventive strategies can be used to ward off later problems. Among these is use of a pacifier. Modern pacifiers are carefully shaped and contribute little to malocclusion, or dental deformities.

2. Look for Sources of Insecurity

Parents might look at possible sources of insecurity in a

thumb-sucking child and try to make sure that home and school experiences aren't contributing to the problem.

3. Ignore It

Active ignoring may be beneficial in dealing with thumb-sucking children younger than age six. If there's absolutely no parental reaction, the child may drop the habit.

4. Limit the Behavior

Furthermore, parents can limit the time of day during which a child can suck his thumb. As an example, a child could suck his thumb during a ten-minute period starting on the hour. If he doesn't suck his thumb during the last fifty minutes of the hour, he earns a reward. At first, the ten-minute period for sucking could be every hour. Later on, the period for sucking might be once every two hours. Once the habit is broken during daytime hours, the strategy can be tried at night.

5. Change the Habit

Like many habits, thumb sucking can become automatic. To change a habit, a person must be aware of doing it. A number of strategies can foster this awareness in a child. One is verbal reminders. Another is putting a bitter-tasting substance on the thumb. Some children become aware of their habit by being made to stand in front of a mirror while sucking their thumbs.

A number of children suck their thumbs only when they're holding a valued object, such as a blanket or a teddy bear. In such cases, taking away the object may reduce thumb sucking.

In general, restrictive strategies like using mittens or gloves or binding the child's arm are inadvisable, except among older children who specifically request those tactics.

6. Use Dental Appliances — Only If Necessary

If there's evidence of a malocclusion in a child, various dental appliances can be used to correct the problem. The child will usually resist, but this strategy should be pursued to avoid long-term damage.

Nail Biting

Nail-biting doesn't necessarily lead to significant medical problems, but many intense and chronic nail biters are ashamed of their nails.

Consequently, they become uncomfortable in certain social situations.

1. **Eliminate Role Models**

   This habit can be prevented by eliminating nail-biting role models. Children can be taught that when a nail breaks off, they can use a scissors or file to smooth the jagged edge.

2. **Use a Chart**

   Most youngsters in middle childhood or adolescence don't like the results of nail biting and become motivated to overcome the habit. Keeping a tally sheet of nail-biting behaviors can help to decrease them. Children carry a little card and mark every time they put a finger in their mouth. The marks are totaled each day and put on a chart, which shows whether the habit is subsiding.

3. **Give Rewards**

   As with other habits, this one might benefit from a reward system for improvements. Parents can specify certain times of the day when the children can engage in nail biting and other times when they'll be rewarded for not doing so. Another intervention strategy that often works—more for females than for males—is to use a manicure as a way to teach them good nail care and hygienic habits with their nails. It can also be used as a reward with a significant period of discontinuing the nail biting. Manicures can be given by a parent, or cosmetology schools often have students who need to practice giving manicures for a nominal charge.

4. **Teach Alternative Behaviors**

   Nail biting is triggered by anxiety, tension, and boredom. Children should be taught to deal with these feelings with more acceptable methods, such as relaxation.

Lying

Lying is among the most intense forms of childhood rebellion. Most parents become distraught and angry when they catch their children breaching the truth. In many families, if a child is ever going to receive corporal punishment, it's likely to be for lying.

Why do children lie? In young children, lying isn't malicious or rebellious. It's a manifestation of the way in which they perceive the world and fail to distinguish between reality and fantasy. For older youngsters, lying can be a symptom of a disrupted and chaotic parent-child relationship. In relationships that do not foster openness, frankness, honesty, and trustworthiness, children often lie.

As with other forms of misbehavior, lying is learned. Children of parents who lie often follow suit. Some children lie because they're angry and want to seek revenge or retaliate against their parents by making them endure the anguish of catching them in a lie. In some cases, children lie because they've been punished excessively for telling the truth. Others find that dishonesty is a way of fulfilling a particular desire or giving themselves something in fantasy that they lack in reality.

Children can be set up to lie. When parents ask children questions to which the answers are already known, the youngster may lie defensively. Other children find lying exciting and become enthralled and delighted with their parent's reactions to their untruths. Lying also serves as a defense for inadequate performance.

The literature and psychological experience reveal a number of different solutions for preventing lying and dealing with it when it occurs.

1. Develop an Open Relationship

An ounce of prevention is worth a pound of cure when it comes to childhood lying. By using a family council, openness, honesty, and realistic consequences, it's possible to establish a family atmosphere in which children can calmly express and understand their problems and frustrations. In such an atmosphere, parents are alert to the early signs of anger, resentment, or hostility that can lead to lying. Also, if consequences are equitable and not excessive, the probability of lying is reduced.

2. Eliminate Inappropriate Models

Children learn to lie from others, particularly from their parents. The father who gloats because he was able to sneak an item past a cashier without paying for it isn't setting a good example. When the phone rings and a mother says, "If it's Jane, tell her I'm not home," the youngster soon learns it's okay to tell little white lies. Set examples of honesty and candor, and examine your tendencies to exaggerate or deny mistakes.

3. Avoid Dramatic Confrontations

Avoid confronting children at the time you discover they've lied. That's when they will be particularly vulnerable, defensive, and most likely to lie again. Discussing the issue later, when things have calmed down, is a better idea. Lecturing, condemning, name-calling, and threatening will only result in fear, anger, and an increased probability of lying.

4. Try Reciprocal Lying
Younger children tell fanciful, colorful lies to impress people. You can sometimes end this tactic by exposing the child to the same thing. Tell them rich, lively tales that are total fabrications, and thereby make the child realize the folly of fibbing. Often this reciprocation will end the tall tales.

5. Use Paradoxical Consequences
With older children who lie persistently, a paradoxical strategy sometimes works. It must, however, be used with caution. Every time you catch your children in a lie, compliment them on how ingenious the dishonesty is. Then give an insignificant reward such as a raisin, a paper clip, or a green stamp. For children who lie to obtain attention, this paradoxical behavior often thwarts their motivation.

6. Declare Open Season on Lying
Another dramatic approach to lying is to hold a family council and suggest that everyone lie to each other all the time. The children have to agree. Also, decide that whenever family members get fed up with lying, they should stop. Before long, the children learn that dishonesty is not the best policy at home, especially when everyone else in the family is lying to them as well. When children are on the receiving end, they view things quite differently. This is a controversial approach, however, that many families find unacceptable.

7. Enforce Lying with Consequences
This strategy works quite well for young children who lie to receive attention. These youngsters may tell stories about getting into fights, beating up other children, and seeing monsters in the neighborhood. One way to deal with this is to determine what the natural outcome of such a lie might be and enforce an appropriate consequence.

For example, children who boast about being the big, tough bullies who beat up every child in the neighborhood need to have more constructive outlets for their energy. They should be assigned extra chores, such as scrubbing the floor or raking the lawn.

8. Don't Inflate Incidents

Lying and other immoral actions can cause catastrophic reactions in parents. They jump to the worst possible conclusions. They visualize their child as a felon, a psychopath, or a member of organized crime. They also may conclude that they're failures as parents because they have malicious children. Again, be realistic. Lying children do not necessarily become criminals.

9. Avoid Double Jeopardy

Parents need to be careful not to increase the probability of lying. If every mistake or poor judgment made by the child results in punishment, the likelihood of lying increases. In addition, if punishments tend to be severely aversive and unbearable, lying will likely get worse. So, to solve the problem, punish only the major lies and keep the consequences realistic. Mildly aversive consequences used consistently will reduce lying.

10. Get at the Basic Cause

Sometimes it's necessary, especially with frequent liars, to get to the bottom of the dishonest behavior. In other words, determine what triggers the lying, so steps can be taken not only to deal with it when it happens but also to prevent it from happening again.

Certain youngsters with low self-esteem brag and exaggerate so they can receive attention and admiration. This allows them to feel better about themselves. In some cases, children lie to protect others. They're afraid that if they don't lie, they'll be rejected by their peer group. There are also children for whom lying becomes a self-fulfilling prophecy. Because of previous dishonesty, they've been labeled as liars.

Some siblings are self-centered and narcissistic and lie to get things for themselves in a relatively easy manner. In these cases, the child needs new social skills.

11. Deal with Cheating

Cheating is a form of lying, and many children up to the age of six or seven cheat regularly at games. They're so wrapped up in their own world that they use whatever strategies they can to come out on top. In such cases, chronic cheating can become a serious problem.

The way to deal with cheating may vary depending on the cause. Children constantly exposed to cheaters will follow their example, particularly if the model is a parental one. Some children cheat because they've acquired an all-or-nothing philosophy from their parents, one reminiscent of the old football adage, "Winning isn't the most important thing. It's the only thing."

Some children cheat for attention, and ignoring the behavior will be effective. Other times, it may work to say, "I'm not willing to continue playing since you cheat. When you stop cheating, we'll play some more." Finally, some youngsters cheat because winning is a way of bolstering their ego. They may feel like failures, and in order to feel better, they need to win at any cost. Children like this can be helped to gain success in other ways. They can also learn to change some of their inner dialogue. For example, while victory is nice, it's okay not to win all the time. Parents can help their children have greater self-confidence and self-esteem by acknowledging their strengths and positive attributes. Cheating can sometimes be prevented by carefully discussing the rules and controversial items before playing games. Noncompetitive activities are likely to yield greater satisfaction and provide less temptation to cheat.

12. Try the Bibliotherapy

Some children who lie can be helped by listening to stories that illustrate the virtues and advantages of telling the truth. These stories shouldn't be highly moralistic, because then children will tune them out. Instead, the message should be simple and straightforward with no preaching.

Here are three good books about lying.

Brink, Carol. *The Bad Times of Irma Baumlein*. New York: Macmillan, 1972.

Gardner, Richard A. "The $ Lie." In *Dr. Gardner's Stories about the Real World*. New York: Prentice Hall, 1972.

Ness, Evaline. *Sam, Bangs, and Moonshine*. Austin, Texas: Holt, Rinehart & Winston, 1966.

Ask your librarian or search online for more stories to illustrate this concept

13. Check It Out

Oftentimes it is beneficial for parents to actually check out the stories that their children or adolescents are telling them. This needs to be done with a fair amount of caution and an indication to the child or teenager that the parent is intending to follow up. This does two things. First, it provides the child with another opportunity to "come clean." Second, it allows the parent to corroborate information from another source and determine an appropriate apology if the situation calls for it or an appropriate consequence for the behavior. Part of the consequence for lying may be that the parents are going to engage in random "checking it out" behavior for a certain period. Having these conditions present may deter a child or adolescent from lying.

Swearing

Children like to feel big and tough. Swearing can produce such dramatic results that they often are encouraged to continue doing it. A horrified response from parents and teachers is sheer delight for many children. In other words, children swear primarily because of the attention it brings them. A number of strategies can be effective in dealing with this problem.

1. **"Please Repeat What You Said"**

   Every time children swear or use unacceptable language, their parents can say they didn't understand and ask them to repeat it. Do this at least twice in a calm, matter-of-fact manner, showing no trace of anger, irritability, or embarrassment—reactions the youngster would expect.

2. **Enumerate**

   In using this strategy, calmly sit with the children and ask them to list as many "bad" words as they know. When they're finished, walk away, giving absolutely no feedback. The message is simple: These words are trivial and not worth getting upset about.

3. **Don't Be a Model**

   Parents who use profanity will likely pass that habit on to their offspring. Watch your language, especially in front of the children.

4. **Ignore It**

   Ignoring is a strategy that works quite well with obnoxious behaviors like swearing. Withhold all attention from the child who swears, remembering that ignoring is an effective but slow-acting, strategy.

5. **Refrain from Panic**

   Don't catastrophize when your children engage in obnoxious behaviors. Swearing is one behavior that parents can find embarrassing, particularly when it occurs in public. But swearing is usually a temporary phenomenon for children that doesn't reflect adversely on the quality of parenting they've received. Keep a realistic attitude about swearing.

6. Impose a Fine

A fine can help some children reduce swearing and obscenity. Tell children that every time they use unacceptable language, it will mean a nickel fine. Other negative consequences might include loss of TV privileges or spending time in isolation.

7. Question the Meaning

When a child uses a profane word or phrase, ask for an explanation in a matter-of-fact, curious manner. For an attention-seeking child, this response defeats the goal of the cursing.

8. Explore Underlying Causes

For some children, swearing is their way of communicating frustration. They may have no other constructive method for ventilating negative feelings and releasing tension. Seek out their covert feelings rather than react to the overt expressions.

9. Reward Improvement

For children who swear a lot, use a charting program to reward the decreasing occurrence of such behavior. Once a baseline has been set, reward the child with a star or check for falling below that norm. As the youngster gradually gains control over proper language, reduce the allowable norm. At agreed-on intervals, exchange stars or checks for a meaningful reward or privilege.

10. Find Alternative Words

With this strategy, encourage the child to use more creative words in place of unacceptable ones. Some may use "blank-blank." Others may find an imaginative expression of their own, such as "shuckleberries."

11. Create No-Swearing Zones

Some children can be helped to overcome the profanity habit by being told that certain language is permissible only in particular areas of the house. If they're in that area, they can use the word. If not, they must say something else. This way, they'll learn optional ways of expressing their anger and eventually may drop their profanity.

12. Keep Records

This is a cooperative method of checking on swearing and obscenities. The offender and the parents each have a card with the days of the week along the left-hand side. Every time the unacceptable language is used, put a check mark on the card. Ask your child to do the same. Keep separate records for several days, then compare notes. The effectiveness of this strategy is twofold. First, record-keeping in and of itself often reduces the bad habit. Second, the fact that this is a cooperative venture informs the child that you really are interested in helping, and communicates that she is okay but her behavior is not.

13. Feign Deafness

Sometimes swearing is engaged to seek attention as stated previously. Under these circumstances, don't overreact; in fact, carry on the conversation or activity as if you are deaf and do not hear the swearing at all. This is a recommended method for swearing that has become a typical part of the child's vocabulary.

Procrastination and Dawdling

Some experts say that procrastination can be a good thing, as long as we're subconsciously working on a problem, or "writing in our minds." With children, however, this often isn't the case.

Some children move at a different rate of speed. They may "march to the same beat of the drummer," just more slowly. However, slowpokes and chronic latecomers are irritating to deal with. A child of ten who procrastinates, dawdles, postpones, and is tardy, often grows up to be an adult with the same characteristics. These are the people who are constantly late for appointments, if they show up at all. They seldom do what they're supposed to do on time.

Being late and not finishing tasks on time may reflect anger. Some children may be afraid to openly express disagreement or hostility. They may never show defiance, but still cause parents frustration because they're careless, late, and sloppy.

Some children use the issue of time as a battleground for expressing rebellion and defiance. They feel locked in a power struggle with their parents. Inactivity is one of their most powerful weapons.

Highly anxious and nervous children tend to be worrisome and fearful of new situations. They may try to avoid scary situations by always being late.

Procrastination can lead to interpersonal problems in adolescence and adulthood. Parents should deal with this problem assertively and not let it go undisciplined. Since it's a problem that may not respond well to ignoring, other strategies are recommended.

1. Model Correctly

Parents who procrastinate and dawdle usually have children of the same ilk. To deal effectively with slowpoke offspring, you must be on time and do things when they're supposed to be done.

2. Allow for Natural Consequences

Don't let the child get away with delay tactics. Make sure the slowpoke suffers appropriate consequences. First, it's important to assess the situation in which the misbehavior occurs and decide what would be a logical, natural discipline.

For example, if the child is a particularly slow eater, set a time limit. When it's been reached, remove all food and dishes from the table. The time limit should be reasonable—perhaps twenty to thirty minutes—and should be administered calmly, nonchalantly, and matter-of-factly. In addition, allow the child no food between meals. This will help her realize that dawdling may lead to hunger.

To deal with the child who's a slow dresser, two natural consequences can be used. Older youngsters can simply be left at home. Younger ones can be firmly but calmly placed in a car and told to get dressed en route to the destination.

Or a time limit can be set. For instance, instruct the child to be ready to leave by ten o'clock. If he isn't ready, he is either left behind or taken to the car, whatever the state of dress.

3. Have Appropriate Expectations

Many child-parent conflicts develop unnecessarily because parents don't have an appropriate appreciation of the rate at which children develop. Children gradually acquire the concept of time. They often do not understand that concept fully until they reach the age of nine, ten, or eleven. Before that, they don't comprehend the linear model of time. They don't see it as a sequential process that travels at a fixed rate. In some cases, they view it as a cyclic phenomenon and think that if they miss an opportunity, they'll have it again.

4. Use an Ounce of Prevention

Routines and rituals established early in childhood set the model for continuing to do things within a reasonable amount of time. At an early age, allow children reasonable but not excessive amounts of time to finish their meals, dress, clean up their rooms, and so on. Timers help with young children.

5. Encourage Helpful Self-Talk

For children who are chronic procrastinators, offer appropriate examples of self-instruction and reward. For example, encourage the child to say out loud: "I'm tired, but I can do it anyway because I'll feel better when it's done." "It's hard to get going, but I know that it feels great when I am finished." "If I hurry and dress on time, my family won't be angry with me."

6. Give Rewards

Encourage children to make better use of their time and avoid stalling by being sure that positive consequences occur when they move at a reasonable rate. Compliment the child for being on time. Offer rewards for completing tasks or being ready on time. Children who have difficulty getting out of bed, for example, could receive a favorite breakfast for getting up on schedule.

7. Reward Approximations

Some children appear lazy and inactive but may be black-and-white or all-or-nothing thinkers. If they don't do something perfectly the first time, they don't want to do it at all. Children like this need to be told that perfection is not expected. They also need to receive rewards for approximations of the final or target behavior.

8. Deal with Indecisiveness

Some children who appear to be procrastinators are actually indecisive. They're afraid to make a decision, fearing they'll be wrong. A three-step strategy deals with this problem. In the first stage, the child identifies as many solutions as possible. In the second, he evaluates them, determining what the consequences might be. After deciding which solutions have the most merit, he chooses one, knowing that if it doesn't work there are other options.

9. Use a Timer

Kitchen timers often work well with procrastinators. The timer itself can serve as a cue reminding the child that certain responsibilities and routines need to be pursued. The timer can become the reminder, instead of the nagging parent.

10. Use Written Reminders

A written reminder of what needs to be done and when it needs to be done is often more effective than a verbal reminder. Use dry-erase boards in kitchens or eating areas for daily reminders. Verbal reminders may soon be forgotten, but the visual reminder is always present.

11. Fix an Amount of Time

Children need to learn that if routine chores and responsibilities aren't performed during the allocated time, they must still be done, but during playtime or fun time.

Temper Tantrums

Temper tantrums can be habit-forming. Children who have a low level of tolerance for frustration and throw frequent tantrums often become adults who do the same in a more grown-up fashion. For this reason, emotional self-control must be learned and practiced in childhood.

We offer twelve suggestions to use when dealing with children who throw temper tantrums. One or more of these strategies may be helpful to you.

1. Remove the Audience

With this strategy, the person for whose benefit the tantrum is thrown leaves the area quickly and calmly. With a very young child, it's important to go just far enough away that the youngster is aware of the absence, but near enough to watch out for the child's well-being. If it's not possible to leave the scene, simply turn your back on the children and say nothing. At home, the bathroom strategy discussed earlier can be used. If several people are present, all of them must use the ignoring strategy or it won't work.

2. Remove the Child

Another way to deal with this problem is to isolate the child through the use of time-out procedures. When tantrums begin, move the child to an isolation area until the tantrum subsides. Then the child can return to the group situation with no mention of the misbehavior.

3. Maintain a Positive Attitude

Many parents encourage tantrums by giving in to them to avoid embarrassment. They feel their child's upset is their fault, and that adults will judge them adversely. So they give in to the tantrum. But giving in only guarantees that the misconduct will be repeated.

Parents need to remind themselves that they aren't raising children to please others. They should impart their values and beliefs to their offspring, even if it means dealing with disapproval from other parents.

4. Set a Good Example

Parents who throw tantrums often have children who do the same. Tantrums aren't restricted to children. We've all seen what happens to adults who miss a key shot in a tennis game or a two-foot putt that costs them a golf match. Some adults throw full-blown tantrums while shopping or driving. If parents expect to reduce the frequency of such behavior in their children, they must set an example.

5. Defuse the Buildup

Some parents insist that temper tantrums are unprovoked and unplanned, but that's usually not the case. A child may harbor small resentments and irritations that haven't been discussed or vented. Then a low-grade perpetual grumpiness can explode into a fit of rage.

Although children may not always be able to verbalize their growing anger, parents may be able to read early signs of trouble and defuse them through reflective or empathic communication. For instance, you might say, "You seem down in the dumps today. Did anything happen at school?" That may give the child the go-ahead to begin talking about what's bothering her. Or she may deny that anything is wrong and continue sulking. But even if the latter occurs, an acknowledgment of feelings may help defuse the potential explosion.

6. Release Angry Energy

Some children without particularly well-developed verbal skills need to release anger through physical activities or relaxation. Allow running or hitting such objects as sofa cushions. On occasion, relaxation techniques like deep-breathing exercises or visualizing a favorite vacation (e.g., the beach) may help dissipate the inner turmoil.

7. Enhance Expression of Anger

For some youngsters, temper tantrums occur because they don't know how else to express their anger. In such cases, the child needs to learn to be assertive without throwing a tantrum. Discuss the child's angry feelings rather than using punishment.

8. Give a Judicious Reward for Improvement

Children who throw tantrums can be rewarded for any small improvement, such as throwing fewer fits during a given time. As children learn to control their tempers, the parameters will be gradually increased. For instance, a child who throws ten tantrums an hour might first be rewarded for only having half that many, and then a third as many. And when a parent notices that a child has handled a particularly frustrating situation without losing control, a compliment is in order.

9. Use Behavior Reversal and Role-Playing

Reenact an upsetting and explosive situation by taking the role of the child and demonstrating alternative ways of dealing with the frustration. Then ask the child to role-play the situation again with a new set of behaviors. This should be practiced several times, and generously praise the child for successful enactment.

10. Encourage Self-Talk

Children, like adults, learn to control their behavior by controlling their thinking. If children are able to tell themselves, "It's frustrating not to get what I want right away, but I can learn to wait my turn," that will help delay gratification.

11. Teach Problem Solving

The likelihood of a tantrum can be reduced if children know how to solve problems. If they're confident that they can solve interpersonal issues, they're much less likely to throw tantrums. They need to learn how to identify problems, develop a variety of strategies for solving them, explore the pros and cons of each strategy, and, finally, carry out a plan.

12. Record It

When a child is engaging in a temper tantrum, ask them to please put the behavior on pause because you want to be sure to record this event for future reference and to show friends and family when they come over. Once you start the audiotape or the camera, instruct the child, "Okay, now it's okay to resume. Please continue. Oh, I think that you can do better than that. Oh, you were doing such a good job before I got the camera I wished I would've had it first." When you can see a child's behavior escalating to the point where a tantrum may in fact be on the horizon, have the camera handy so you can record it. Children usually do not want to be embarrassed by their behavior or have it recorded for other people to see. A variation of this strategy has the child listen to or watch the tantruming on the videotape once there is a moment of calm.

Spitting

Spitting can be an annoying and unsanitary habit that children pick up from watching adults. Toddlers often spit water because parents do it when brushing their teeth. Tobacco-chewing fathers may have boys who continually turn their heads to the side and spit. In extreme cases, children spit at other people.

Some parents faced with this problem believe in the revised Golden Rule: "Do unto others as they do unto you." They spit back. We do not encourage this strategy because spitting can be an aggressive, humiliating, and demeaning act. We recommend several more effective techniques.

1. **Don't Be a Model**
   Parents who spit have children who copy that behavior. If these parents will make a habit of using tissues or a handkerchief for disposing of excess mucus, children will generally follow suit.

2. **Try Satiation**
   Another successful strategy is to require the child to fill a cup to a certain level with spittle. Immediately after the child spits in an unacceptable manner, present the cup. Tell the child to spit until the cup is full. This may not work the first time, but sooner or later the child will grow tired of this consequence.

3. **Try Isolation**
   Spitting is often attention-seeking behavior. If it's punished by isolation, the child will not achieve the goal.

4. **Ignore It Actively**
   Isolated spitting incidents are often best dealt with by ignoring the child. Active ignoring consists of no visual, verbal, or tactile attention. This strategy isn't recommended if a child spits at a person.

5. **Understand the Dynamics**
   When children spit at someone, ask them to describe what hap-

pened and the reasons for it. For example, "I spit at Susie because …." If children have difficulty verbalizing those feelings, they should be told to write them down. If they can't get in touch with the anger or fear behind the act, then it might be best to openly confront them. You might say, "Jimmy, when you spit at Susie, you tell me that you really don't like her, but also that you feel bad about yourself."

Chapter Five

Emotional Problems

Fears and Phobias

All children have irrational fears. They can include fear of water, heights, spiders, separation, and going to school. Handled properly, these fears needn't be debilitating. Here are some techniques that may help children deal with fears and phobias.

1. **Resolve *Your* Fears**

   Parents who are fearful and phobic often have children with similar traits. If you have an unrealistic fear, the first step in helping a phobic child may be for you to resolve your anxiety. In dealing with simple fears (for example, fear of insects), you can set up your own modeling program. In more severe cases (for example, fear of eating), professional help may be needed.

2. **Use Gradual Exposure**

   One effective way to help children deal with unrealistic fears is to use a desensitization treatment program. This means exposing the child gradually to the feared object. For example, if the child is afraid of going in the lake, the family first determines how close their youngster can get to the water without undue anxiety. When the child appears comfortable, the family can move a step closer while playing ball or engaging in some other activity. It may take ten or twenty days of exposure before the child feels brave enough to enter the water.

3. **Test Reality**

   An approach that can be traumatic but effective is to let a child experience the frightening object all at once until the anxiety disappears. For example, if the child is afraid to go on a playground, a parent could make the youngster stay until the discomfort subsides. Or the child could be pulled into knee-deep water and held there until the fear goes away. While this strategy may work, it can be difficult to pursue, and we don't generally recommend it.

4. Stay Cool

A calm, confident, and relaxed parent can help children allay fears. Fear often develops because of incorrect and insufficient knowledge. Children need to be reassured that virtually everyone experiences fear or anxiety at some time, so they shouldn't be overly concerned about it. That thought, conveyed comfortably, can go a long way toward reducing the intensity of a child's anxious reaction to a particular stimulus.

5. Don't Threaten

At some time or another, parents may imagine abandoning their children. They may wish someone would snatch their children out of the grocery store. Of course, parents don't really want that to happen. They're simply human, and might be irrationally angry, just like children. Children, on the other hand, have a natural fear of being abandoned or rejected by parents. Therefore, if parents feel intense resentment, they should keep it to themselves. A threat of abandonment, even though not genuine, can result in a high level of fear and anxiety for a child.

6. Be There

When you tell your child you'll meet him after school, it's important to keep that promise, and to be on time. To be late can alarm a child and stimulate fear of abandonment.

For particularly anxious children, establish a predictable daily routine. With toddlers, anxiety increases when other children's parents have come for them, but theirs are late. If you can't keep the appointment with older children, reassure them in some way, like leaving a message on a family communication board or a note with the teacher, explaining the circumstances. In some cases, it might be possible to have a neighbor greet children and assure them that nothing dramatic has happened.

7. Prepare for Separation

Some parents sneak away when children are asleep or at school. Others leave on vacations without telling their child what they're doing, leaving that task to a babysitter or friend. This strategy often creates anxiety and anger.

Always prepare your children for separation, regardless of the children's ages, no matter how difficult it may seem. The message conveyed is that the leave of absence will be a brief one. Also, preparation for an extended separation should begin weeks in advance. With toddlers and preschoolers, it's helpful to communicate the meaning of the separation using their play materials. For instance, when going on a vacation, a toy airplane can be used to explain what will take place.

8. Find the Underlying Cause

In helping fearful and insecure children, try to discover the underlying reasons for the problem. As stated earlier, children usually learn through imitation. Since parents are children's chief models, your displays of fear may be duplicated by your child. A number of scenarios are possible. Parents who are insecure in other ways may also promote a similar insecurity. Parents who are excessively critical or demanding often have fearful and timid children who feel inadequate and unappreciated. Parents who fight a great deal may promote insecurity and fear in their children.

Some children become fearful as a way of dealing with feelings they believe are unacceptable. Others have violently aggressive feelings or vivid sexual desires, and feel they'll be punished for them. Younger children in particular project these feelings onto others. The children come to faithfully believe people are angry with them, hate them, and want to hurt them, so they become fearful and insecure.

Fears may also be rooted in trauma. A child may have had a frightening experience involving a high place, an animal, thunder, or lightning. Children may generalize these fears and become afraid of all animals, all high places, or all storms, even though there is no realistic basis for it.

9. Use Bibliotherapy

Try exposing fearful children to stories in which other children learn to overcome fears. Children have a tendency to identify with heroes in stories. If a hero successfully and courageously faces what is feared, children also may learn to do so. A trip to a library or bookstore should be helpful in finding books written for children about various fears and how heroes overcome them.

Here are a few examples.

Brett, Doris. *Annie Stories.* New York: Workman, 1987.

Campbell-Murphy, Elspeth. *God Cares When I'm Worried.* Elgin, Ill.: Chariot Books, 1983.

Dragonwagon, Crescent. *Will It Be Okay?* New York: Harper & Row, 1977.

Duczman, Linda. *The Babysitter.* Milwaukee: Raintree Editions; Chicago: Children's Press, 1977.

Dutro, Jack. *Night Light: A Story for Children Afraid of the Dark.* New York: Magination Press, 1991.

Goode, Diane. *I Hear a Noise.* New York: Dutton, 1988.

Griffith, Helen V. *Alex Remembers.* New York: Greenwillow Books, 1983.

10. Try Early Prevention

The importance of preparing children for separation was discussed previously. However, children also need to be prepared for regular, predictable developmental stresses, such as a visit to the doctor or dentist. Before such a trip have your child accompany you to your appointment. When the doctor is done, comment on how good you feel and how glad you are that you both went. If, for example, your child is frightened by dogs, strategies for relating to friendly dogs should be developed.

11. Harness the Power of Positive Thinking

Children's feelings are influenced by their thinking. If children can learn to talk common sense to themselves and keep fears in perspective, they'll feel less afraid. They need to be encouraged to think and speak positive thoughts to themselves. They can say, for instance, "Everyone is afraid once in a while. I can deal with this scary thing. It won't hurt me."

Variations of positive approaches that are successful with adults can be used with children. For example, tell them to clap their hands together very loudly and shout "Stop!" when they have a frightening thought. Later on, they can do this quietly in their heads. Next, they can learn positive self-talk and recall an image or event that's warm and encouraging. This imagined event can then be used to deal with fears.

12. Practice Makes Perfect

Children fearful of objects or situations can overcome their fears through practice. For example, they may use puppets to play-act fear of heights, dogs, water, and so on. They can also practice approaching feared objects by using their imagination. By using puppets or creative thinking, children can practice how they'll handle varieties of fears when they actually occur. Moreover, it's important that adults praise and reward children for engaging in this rehearsal approach.

13. Teach Them to Relax

Like adults, children can't be relaxed and nervous at the same time. The two states of mind are mutually exclusive. Relaxation counteracts anxiety. Therefore, children can overcome fears by learning how to relax.

Relaxation isn't something acquired at birth—and it doesn't come naturally. It's a skill acquired through practice. Ultimately, if children practice systematic relaxation long and hard enough, they'll learn to do it simply by using a key word.

There are a number of relaxation strategies that children can easily learn. Some are primarily breathing exercises. Others require systematically contracting and relaxing certain muscle pairs. Generally speaking, most children can acquire appropriate relaxation responses if they practice twice a day for about two weeks. The goal is for a child to be relaxed, but also alert and attentive.

14. Accentuate the Positive

As with much problem behavior, the consequences are critical in determining progress. Parents need to be alert for small signs of increased courage in children who are generally shy or fearful, and offer praise, hugs, and kisses.

Parents shouldn't rely on all-or-nothing philosophies of reward. Children need to receive positive feedback, praise, and compliments for small successes. This can be given both verbally and with a tangible reward, such as money earned through a point system. Children who constantly complain about phobias could be praised for fewer complaints.

Parents need to be careful not to reward or punish fearful behavior. They need to determine whether a child's apprehensive behavior is bringing its own subtle rewards, or whether additional coping skills and support are needed. Although parental reassurance is important, it's useless if it occurs only for fearful behavior. To avoid this trap, display support at all times, not just in fearful situations.

15. Use a Superhero

Oftentimes it is difficult for children to describe the fears or phobias they are experiencing using words. While drawing pictures or acting things out may be advantageous, another possible strategy is using a storytelling strategy involving a superhero. Children can tell what their fears are via this third person and then add as part of the story what the superhero would do to conquer the fears and phobias. Sometimes children will come up with something that is outlandish because many superheroes have exceptional powers that children will not be able to duplicate. You can then take their ideas of what the superhero would do and create something for the child to do to combat their fears and phobias.

Soiling

Although most preschool children have adequate bowel control, accidents happen. Habitual soiling after completion of successful toilet training, however, is often a symptom of a physical or emotional disorder. In general, the older the child, the more serious the problem.

Soiling may be an internalized form of rebellion, anger, or hostility. It may indicate highly anxious and perfectionistic youngsters who've been victims of strict toilet-training procedures. In contrast to many behavioral problems, soiling, or encopresis, requires professional consultation if the child doesn't respond quickly to common-sense approaches like those presented in the following pages.

1. Have Matter-of-Fact Discussions
A child who continues to soil may be indicating regression and a desire to be coddled. Frequently this behavior occurs after the birth of a rival sibling. A major danger is overreaction by a parent who excessively punishes a child, then feels guilty and follows with an emotional apology. The attention a child receives after punishment can actually serve as a reward for soiling. When soiling occurs, the child needs to be told calmly that "It was okay to have bowel movements in your pants when you were little and didn't know better, but you're bigger and older now, and we want you to use the toilet."

2. Allow Natural Consequences
When older children soil, they should be required to clean up their mess and empty it into the toilet. Then they should soak and scrub all soiled clothing and bathe themselves. These activities should be done with minimal parental involvement. Once the children learn that "dirty work" follows soiling, the problem often ends.

3. Employ Realistic Toilet Training
Children whose parents stress perfectionism often develop encopresis. These parents should take heed. It's important to take

a casual and tolerant approach to toilet training. Accidents should be accepted and should not result in punishment. Instead, natural consequences should be used.

4. Use a Reward System

Children who soil mildly often respond to a charting system. This is similar to the process used in dealing with enuresis, or bed-wetting. A child is rewarded for a clean day.

Some manipulative youngsters may remove their soiled underwear and destroy it, perhaps by flushing it down the toilet. Then they put on a clean pair and act as if nothing happened. To monitor this scenario, parents can put numbers on their child's underwear in indelible ink. Each morning, the parent notes which underpants were worn and checks again at the end of the day to see if the child is wearing the same pair. If the clean day is legitimate, the child gets a reward. As progress continues, the rewards are given for two successful days, three, and so on. An alternative method is to reward the child for using the toilet. In the case of severe problems, both approaches can be used together.

5. Pay Attention to Anger and Hostility

Many children soil because it's the only avenue allowed for negative expression. This occurs when parents are rigid, authoritarian, and intolerant, and stifle childhood expression. This problem can be alleviated by using empathic communication approaches and allowing the child to vent a range of feelings. Parents should make sure that venting of feelings doesn't become violent or destructive.

6. Use Charting

In coping with soiling, daily record-keeping is essential. The child could help by recording both accidents and successes. Post results in a conspicuous place. Simple record-keeping in and of itself often serves to decrease undesirable behaviors and increase desirable ones. Charting heightens awareness of the problem and results in greater self-control.

7. Use Logical Consequences

Although we don't advocate penalties for soiling, some parents have successfully used a combined reward-and-punishment procedure. In these cases, the child is rewarded for appropriate bowel movements and experiences logical consequences for inappropriate ones.

Some logical consequences may be helpful, such as making a

child bathe or shower immediately after soiling. During the process, the child shouldn't receive attention other than necessary supervision. By prior arrangement with a teacher, children who soil in the classroom can be asked to clean themselves and change clothes at school, then make up the time they missed.

8. Reduce Fear

Some children acquire a fear of the toilet. This may result from some uncomfortable experience. Whatever the cause, a desensitization approach is recommended. This could mean starting with a potty chair, then moving to a toilet seat, and finally to the actual toilet. In severe cases, professional consultation may be required.

9. Employ Preventive Strategies

Many children who have difficulty with soiling are highly emotional and anxious. They have problems expressing anger and resentment. These youngsters need to acquire alternative ways to deal with their emotions. One such method, discussed previously in this book, is the method of relaxation.

Children who have regular eating habits that include balanced meals with moderate levels of bulk or fiber have fewer problems with soiling. A diet including fresh fruits and vegetables can be advantageous. Also, parents shouldn't refer to fecal matter in a pejorative manner, such as "icky," "dirty," or "messy." To do so may stir fear and disgust in a child and encourage soiling.

10. Pursue Professional Consultation

If soiling doesn't respond to these strategies, consult with a pediatrician to determine if the child has a physical problem. If none is found, the pediatrician should recommend a child psychologist or child psychiatrist experienced in dealing with encopresis.

Sadness

Even very young children can become exceedingly sad and tearful over extended periods of time. They can become withdrawn, apathetic, sensitive, vulnerable, worrisome, irritable, and grumpy, exhibiting temper tantrums and explosiveness.

The vast majority of children who become noticeably unhappy are reacting to some disappointing event or circumstance, such as a failure in school or a relationship problem. Separation from a friend or family, or marital or employment problems, can lead to lowered self-esteem and insecurity.

Usually these feelings subside within a reasonable amount of time. But if they linger, the sadness should be taken seriously. Prolonged feelings of helplessness or hopelessness can lead to self-destructive behavior. In these cases, a child's depression may be due to a biochemical imbalance rather than a response to particular events. For children who have prolonged bouts of depression, seek professional help.

Prior to seeking counseling, a number of strategies can be helpful in dealing with early indications of "the blues."

1. Try an Empathic Response

When children are sad, discouraged, or dejected, one of the most important things they need is understanding. But they often expect parents to intuit what is going on inside and are reluctant to openly disclose their inner feelings and thoughts.

Don't allow this pattern to emerge. When you sense signs of depression, respond with statements such as, "Boy, it must have been a bad day for you. You must have felt bad when you found out that Jimmy was going to move." Don't ask children why they're depressed or tell them to shape up and feel better on their own. Bad feelings won't disappear by being wished away.

2. Be Realistic and Rational

Another approach to dealing with sadness and depression in children focuses more on thoughts than feelings. This approach contends that bad thoughts are related to bad feelings; therefore, if a child is able to think more rationally and realistically, the corresponding feelings will be less intense.

While recognizing the validity of the child's feelings, try to convince him that the event causing despair isn't a catastrophe. For example, they might say to a child whose best friend has moved, "It's disappointing that Jimmy and his family had to move to California. But even though the two of you were special buddies, Jimmy is not the only friend in the world for you. Just as you were able to have a good friendship with Jimmy, you'll be able to have other special friends."

3. Encourage Activity and Exercise

Many adults find that they can work through episodes of depression or discouragement by renewed efforts to avoid dwelling on self-defeating, worrisome experiences. The same is true with children.

In a gentle but direct way, encourage withdrawn, listless children to become more involved in pleasurable pursuits such as athletics or civic work. Like adults, children are better at focusing on only one activity at a time. Therefore, if they're engaged in positive and fulfilling activities, they're less likely to dwell on negative thoughts.

4. Anticipate

Sometimes you may know about an event that may cause sadness, such as a separation, in advance. If children can be prepared for these situations before they occur, they can often adjust with less discomfort. One way to do this is through role-playing. A child who's expecting separation from a parent (for example, because of divorce) can practice ways of communicating with that parent after the separation has occurred. A similar approach might be used when a friend moves.

5. Increase Love and Affection

Children who tend to be sad and depressed often experience intense feelings of insecurity and helplessness. They may feel inadequate and unable to cope. When this happens, parents can increase the amount of unconditional love and affection they give to their children. Sad children, like all children, need to know that they're valued, loved, and wanted. Parents need to continue to give the message of love even if the child doesn't seem responsive to it. And parents should let their children know that they're readily available in times of stress and turmoil.

6. Postpone Consequences

Depression assumes a variety of forms in children and adolescents. Some forms, such as withdrawal and tears, are easily recognized. Others, like irritability and noncompliance, are more difficult to identify. When parents suspect that noncompliance is due to depression, deal with the child's feelings first, before dealing with the behavior. This is a reversal of what's recommended for noncompliance otherwise. But in cases like this, the best time to talk may be at the time of infraction; after children have had a chance to cool down, they may be less likely to share their feelings with parents. Determining whether sadness is at the root of irritability and anger may require a great deal of wisdom and discernment.

7. Prevent Guilt

Depression can result from excessive guilt. A little guilt is a good thing. It enhances a sense of conscience and responsibility, and is a cornerstone of moral behavior. In some families, however, it can be carried to extreme. Be alert to this risk. Don't promote excessive guilt in children.

Many children become sad or depressed because they turn anger and hostility inward. They've learned that it's bad to express anger toward others. To combat this, foster an open expression of feelings.

Children should be able to discuss all feelings, no matter how traumatic, with their parents. Not every expression is acceptable, however. If children become verbally abusive, then discussion can be postponed until they've regained control and can discuss their feelings in a more rational manner.

Some children become depressed because they feel they're powerless to impact the world around them or their own lives. But if children feel adequate and appropriately independent, they gain a sense of satisfaction and purpose. Encourage active problem-solving strategies. At an early age, urge children to make informed choices and to have an active approach to life. Children who develop effective problem-solving strategies early have a lower propensity for depression than those who don't.

Some children develop depressive reactions as a means of gaining attention and sympathy from important people in their lives. When other methods don't work, they begin to explore alternatives such as acting out, soiling, wetting, or overeating.

Other children use self-destructive tendencies as forms of hostility and revenge. They may pull out their hair and eyelashes or engage in head-banging. These injurious actions, often associated with depression, may result from humiliation or rejection. A child with these feelings needs alternative avenues of expression, which usually are established at an early age.

Many youngsters become depressed when they can't cope with stress. Stress may take many forms. It may come from school or from trying to live up to parental expectations and may include symptoms like muscle constriction, sweating, a flushed face, or stuttering.

Children who don't find appropriate solutions for stress may develop depressive symptoms like fatigue and lethargy. Consequently, parents should make their expectations and demands reasonable and appropriate to the ages of their children. If school personnel seem to have unreasonable academic presumptions, parents may need to talk to them about the problem, or consider alternative education.

Depressed children often come from families where there's hostility and conflict between parents. Parents whose relationships include a great deal of discord should seek counseling or deal with it in other ways so as not to affect their children.

8. Foster Self-Esteem and Goal-Directed Activities

Encourage children to develop strong, close relationships with as many people as possible. Children with low self-esteem often become depressed. If children experience success and satisfaction in a number of areas, they're less likely to become depressed. Broaden their academic pursuits to allow success in numerous subjects. To help with a sense of athletic success, children need to experience competency in various sports. Encourage music, acting, and writing activities. For children who are "down in the dumps," activity is essential. Exercise can help, and so can hobbies and building projects. These activities can help direct children toward goals, and teach positive things that they *can* do.

9. Be a Good Model

Children imitate not only their parents' behaviors, but also their attitudes toward life. If parents convey an attitude of helplessness and pessimism, children are likely to acquire the same trait. But active, optimistic, and purposeful parents will set a positive atmosphere at home. Share good feelings and accomplishments with your children. When times are rough, verbalize positive self-talk, such as, "I'm not going to worry about it at this point. It's a rough problem, but I'm sure we'll find a solution."

10. Be Frank and Honest

Many parents are afraid of their own depressive, self-destructive thoughts and, even more, of their children's. As adults, they need to "turn the tables" once in a while and share their feelings, and let children listen to their concerns. This can help children feel needed, and encourage them to talk openly about innermost feelings.

11. Deal with Self-Injury

In mild cases of self-injurious behavior (head-banging, face-slapping, etc.), parents may decide to apply intervention strategies at the outset before consulting a professional. If self-injurious behavior escalates either in frequency or severity, professional consultation is clearly needed.

12. Distinguish Between Long- and Short-Term Goals

Some children become easily discouraged because they don't realize that long-term goals actually take a long time to achieve. They look at the end product and see it as overwhelming after comparing it with where they're at. They become so discouraged and pessimistic that they give up. The child, for example, who wants to become a major-league baseball player, but who has trouble catching a ball, may abandon all efforts. Easily discouraged children can often be helped by pointing out that long-term goals are reached only after successfully achieving a sequence of short-term goals. Similarly, discouraged children need to learn to realize that errors and mistakes aren't failures. Rather they are part of trial-and-error problem-solving strategies.

13. Help Others

Children who tend to be sad and discouraged can be helped by tutoring other people or showing other people how to do something special. By becoming involved in teaching someone else how to do something, they can experience success and divert their attention away from themselves.

14. Encourage Alternate Expression

As stated previously, some children have difficulty verbally expressing things they are feeling sad about or other emotional experiences. Some children are much more comfortable making a drawing about something they are sad about or acting it out in the form of a play. Depending on the interests of their children, parents can suggest these alternative methods of expressing their experience rather than talking about it.

Dealing with Overdependency

Dependent children are recognizable by many behaviors. They may hesitate to do anything without explicit parental approval, seek constant help in doing things, show other signs of immaturity such as whining and crying, and want parents and others to keep them constantly happy and entertained. This kind of behavior is fairly frequent between ages two and five. If it persists beyond that time, parents should intervene in a consistent and deliberate manner.

Many parents tolerate overly dependent children, especially girls. But we strongly encourage dealing with this problem, regardless of the child's gender, by trying one or more of the following ideas.

1. Nip It in the Bud

Like many annoying habits, overdependency is often evident at an early age. Parents can discourage its continuation by helping children meet their own needs, while keeping the youngsters' developmental levels in perspective. Don't do things for children they can do for themselves. Discourage overdependency by encouraging early decision making. Children become independent and self-sufficient only after they're assured that they have parental caring and support. Once children know the backing is there, they're able to venture out on their own.

2. Set an Example

The overly dependent child often has a model with the same personality. Most of us are familiar with a mother who depends on her husband for a solution to every mechanical problem. Some women won't pound a nail to hang a picture or tighten a loose screw on a pot handle. Similarly, we've seen fathers who can prepare nothing edible except a peanut butter and jelly sandwich. Model independence. Don't run to someone else to solve every problem.

3. Determine the Underlying Causes

The problem underlying overdependency is usually related to parental behavior. Some parents are overprotective, especially with their youngest child. They don't want the child to grow up and be independent of them.

Some parents encourage childhood dependency because they feel guilty. For instance, fathers who are often absent because of work responsibilities may foster dependency.

4. Be Consistent

Overdependent children are often whiners. Whining is rewarded when a child forces parents to give in after an initially firm stand. To successfully deal with overdependency, be firm and decisive, but not harsh or cruel. Children need to know that when you say no, there is nothing they can do to change that decision.

5. Ignore the Behavior

When a whining child asks a parent to do something that the child is capable of doing, there's one simple solution: Ignore the behavior. Active ignoring means having no contact with the child whatsoever. It may mean leaving the room. It may also mean exaggerating the ignoring behavior. For example, wearing ear muffs indicates nonverbally to the child that you are not listening to what they are saying. Try having conversations with other family members or even responding to the child who is tantruming in a whisper.

A related strategy is called the "broken record." Say the same thing every time the child makes a demand. For example, you might say, "You can do it." No matter what the child asks you to do, use the same response stated in the same matter-of-fact tone.

Another strategy is to change the subject. While acting as though you aren't hearing anything, comment, "Oh my gosh, I forgot to clean a window."

6. Use Negative Consequences

Parents may decide that ignoring isn't working quickly enough, and turn to the use of negative consequences for overdependency traits like whining, crying, and interrupting. Isolation is a good consequence. Loss of privilege is another.

7. Give Rewards

A reward system can be used in a number of ways to encourage independent behavior. Identify a list of dependent behaviors, and give the child a reward for a decrease in such behaviors. For example, after a baseline has been determined, reward the child for whining fewer than five times during a day. In effect, reward the low frequency of obnoxious behavior. Over time, lower the criterion and give the reward only for a total lack of the misconduct.

This system can also be used to encourage independent behavior. You can identify numerous desirable behaviors on a checklist, and give the child appropriate rewards for their regular occurrence. Or the positive and negative approaches can be combined by giving points for independent action and subtracting them for dependent behavior.

8. Learning Positive Self-Talk

The overdependent child often internalizes immature and self-defeating monologues like "I can't do it" or "I need help." To counter this, urge the child to repeat the independent statements aloud: "I can do it if I take enough time" or "Let me try it myself first, and then if I need help I can ask for it." In this way, youngsters can talk themselves into believing they can handle particular tasks and become more independent.

Sleep Disturbance

Sleep disturbances are complex. Some children have difficulty falling asleep. Others have nightmares or night terrors. Still others wake up periodically. The factors behind these disturbances are difficult to understand. In dealing with them, parents sometimes must walk a narrow line between being indulgent and letting the children sleep with them and being unconcerned and aloof.

If given too much attention for sleep disturbances, a child is encouraged to continue to act helpless and demand care. But cold, rejecting parents may make a child feel insecure, causing even deeper fears.

Sometimes attention isn't the only issue involved. Children may be reliving a traumatic experience. They may have been frightened at bedtime or during the night. Children have been known to be angry with parents and want to hurt or get even with them, so they keep them up at night. Some youngsters develop sleep problems because they regress into a period of wanting to be treated like a baby. Others are simply hungry.

It's especially difficult to deal with sleep disturbances, because most parents are usually half-awake, groggy, and irritable when they occur. These interruptions catch parents at their weakest and most vulnerable moments.

The strategies presented here for dealing with nighttime disturbances can be applied to children ranging in ages from one to fourteen.

1. Gauge Attention

Children who have regular nightmares need parental reassurance. When a child cries out during sleep, wait a specified length of time before doing anything, perhaps five to fifteen minutes. If after that time the child is still awake, go into the child's room and offer brief verbal and physical reassurance. Don't pick the child up, but touch the child instead, and give calm assurance that it's simply been a bad dream. Then say good night and leave the room. We don't recommend ignoring this problem. Giving it measured attention, rather than making a big deal of it, can prevent the disturbance from getting out of hand.

2. Find the Cause

Children who haven't discussed and dealt with negative feelings often have nightmares. Youngsters who are reticent or emotionally constricted may dream as a means of venting or working through their feelings of inadequacy, insecurity, or unresolved anger, revenge, or hatred. If there are many bad dreams, gradually help the child discuss negative feelings, teaching him or her that it's safe to express inner feelings. It may be helpful for the child to act out a nightmare, assuming the role of hero or heroine in overcoming an adversity.

3. Control Stimuli

The experiences and stimulations in a child's day are often manifested in dreams. Children who watch a scary movie, for example, may dream about it. Peer pressure sometimes encourages children to watch movies that scare them. For some children, the thrilling excitement they experience during the movie is rewarding. During the night, however, that exhilaration can come back to haunt them. A strategy for dealing with nightmares of this kind is simply to eliminate their cause—the horror movie.

4. Practice Relaxation

Some children are restless sleepers who toss and turn all night and wake frequently. It may be beneficial for these youngsters to acquire the skill of going back to sleep calmly and peacefully.

For some, initiating fanciful, imaginative, dreamlike processes can be helpful. Most children have vivid imaginations and fantasies they use during the day to make them relaxed, competent, and powerful. For example, young boys or girls may focus on being sports heroes, successful professionals, or actors.

Older children sometimes benefit from simple breathing techniques. For example, they could inhale through their noses and exhale through their mouths. Teenagers find this practice particularly helpful. Adolescents who are awake during much of the night should not use the bed for watching TV, reading, listening to music, or studying. These activities may hinder their ability to relax there so they should do them elsewhere.

Another strategy is to encourage children not to stay in bed for more than fifteen minutes without sleeping. If they aren't sleeping, they should get up, sit in a chair, turn on a light, and begin reading some tedious material. When they begin feeling drowsy, they should get back into bed. If they're still awake in fifteen more minutes, they should repeat the process until it works.

5. Establish a Routine

Many sleeping problems can be avoided by use of regular routines and rituals. There should be a set time for going to bed and getting up even on the weekends. The hour before a child goes to bed should be quiet time. During that time, the child might take a bath, be read to, or be allowed to read nonstimulating, nonfrightening stories. In dealing with all ages, it's important when parents say good night that they leave the room decisively. A parent should avoid pushing a child at bedtime. Forcing children to bed early as discipline only causes them to associate bedtime with something negative.

6. Allow a Night-Light

Some children are afraid of being left alone in their rooms without a light on. Most of the time, leaving a light on in the hallway or having a night-light in the room will suffice. Children are sometimes afraid of shadows or imagined forms in a dimly lit room. Rearranging the room can help. Some youngsters also respond well to a program of rewards for going to sleep in a dimly lit room.

Other children want a light in their room to be left on and can usually sleep satisfactorily in that situation. One strategy is to install a dimmer switch to gradually decrease the light in the room. Or, the child may be given a flashlight to put under the pillow. A child shouldn't be punished for wanting a light on.

When children appear to be primarily frightened of being alone, as opposed to the room's lighting level, a questionable solution to that dilemma is staying with them until they doze off. A better way is to have a pet or favorite stuffed toy in or near the bed.

7. Encourage Positive Thinking

Verbal instructions help children get to sleep. Encourage children to think about pleasant activities or situations before they go to bed. If they're worried about grades or friends, suggest solving the problem together in the morning.

It's sometimes helpful for children to play a game or pretend they're going to put a favorite TV character to sleep with a story they make up. Help children create and verbalize the story. Additionally, tape-record a story and play it back.

8. Make a Dream Catcher

A dream catcher can be made from any kind of materials the child wants and hung over the head of his bed. The child is instructed that this dream catcher will catch all the bad dreams that he may have and replace those bad dreams with good and pleasant dreams. He also needs to know that a dream catcher needs to be cleaned out periodically so that there is room for future bad dreams.

9. Use Sleep Dust

This strategy is related to the "magic lotion" and "anti-itch lotion." It begins with talcum powder. Store the powder in a generic container. The powder can have some additional ingredients such as cornmeal or maybe a tad of pepper or some other granulated spices to add scent to it. The idea is that this is a sleep dust and when it is sprinkled around the child's bed or bedroom or even very lightly sprinkled on her pajamas, it will help her relax and sleep can come more readily. Tell her that this dust will not actually make her go to sleep, but it will provide conditions such as relaxation and regular breathing that will help her to go to sleep.

10. Use an Ounce of Prevention

At bedtime, don't bring up subjects that may be exciting (a vacation, a special trip, a new toy) or upsetting (a potentially frightening visit, a problem at school). Naps shouldn't be close to bedtime. There should be at least thirty to sixty minutes of quiet time before bedtime.

Eating Disturbances

Recently, eating problems in younger children have received considerable professional attention. The four main eating disturbances are pica, obesity, anorexia nervosa, and bulimia.

Pica refers to eating non-nutritional substances like dirt, paint, clay, and plaster, and usually occurs in small children. *Obesity* is overeating resulting in excess body fat. *Anorexia nervosa* is a dangerous form of self-starvation. *Bulimia* refers to an alternating cycle of bingeing followed by purging, including excessive use of diuretics, laxatives, and self-induced vomiting.

Pica

Intervention strategies for pica require thorough medical evaluation and ongoing follow-ups. Pica can lead to lead poisoning, so each case must be followed carefully. Also, the following strategies may be necessary as supplementary approaches.

1. Reduce Stress

Children with pica sometimes are under a great deal of stress and eat inedible items as a way of coping. This stress may be due to irregularity in daily routines. It may be reduced if parents and caretakers emphasize predictability and consistency of routines. Loud noises and fighting may also increase the tendency toward pica. By reducing these stressors, a child's propensity for pica should decrease.

2. Increase Caring

Not surprisingly, children under stress may feel a lack of support or caring. Improving the quality of care, especially emotional support, physical contact, and affection, may reduce a tendency to turn to nonnutritional, inedible.

3. Change the Environment

It may be necessary to move away from areas containing leaded paint or certain kinds of soil. At a minimum, restrict the child's exposure to those items.

4. Improve Nutrition

With the help of a physician or nutritionist, a careful altering of the child's diet may be necessary so deficiencies (for example, vitamins and minerals) can be overcome.

Obesity

Whatever its causes, obesity is a serious problem for children because of its impact on their physical and emotional well-being and self-esteem.

A number of ways are effective in attacking the problem of childhood obesity.

1. Prevent Weight Gain

Since most weight-reduction programs have minimal long-range effects, it seems the best way to eliminate obesity is to prevent it. Many fad diets have temporary weight-reduction results, but are harmful in various ways. Also, statistics show that most weight lost is regained in a relatively short time. Therefore, a number of strategies are needed to help reduce the chances for obesity on a long-lasting basis.

Many parents are constantly tempted to use food as a reward or as a means of easing frustration and anxiety. When children are frustrated, angry, or sad, don't encourage them to eat. Food shouldn't be used as a reward, except in cases of severe difficulties. For example, treats can be used as rewards in the early stages of teaching important self-help skills like toileting. Even then, the habit should be phased out as quickly as possible.

There's increasing evidence that fat children tend to be fat as adults. Children who are overweight by the time they reach age six will probably remain fat from then on. Prevent this condition from occurring in the first place.

Experience shows us that overweight parents tend to have overweight children. This appears to be a function of at least two variables. First, overweight parents tend to fix meals that promote obesity. Second, these parents tend to model overeating.

From early on, parents need to establish a nutritious diet in their household. Although children usually love foods containing fat and refined sugar, the long-range effects of consuming such food can include severe dental problems and obesity. The easiest way to stop a fat-and-sugar craving is to avoid it from the onset. Refined sugars and fats should be used prudently.

Another important ingredient in preventing overeating and obesity is the elimination of feelings of insecurity or inadequacy that often prompt overindulgence in food as a source of contentment. A child who enjoys feelings of success and accomplishment athletically, academically, or with family and peers is unlikely to overeat.

Cultural and familial factors that promote overeating can't be ignored. Many cultures and ethnic groups view food as an important part of family life. Almost everyone has relatives, especially grandmas and aunts, who would be personally offended if their guests refused to eat everything offered them. In several cultural groups, overeating is a ritual. In some families, food consumption is a symbol of affection, caring, and love. But regardless of pressures, nobody should eat in excess. In this respect, it is advantageous to teach children to attend to their body's sensation of being full and their body's sensation of being hungry. Teaching children how to be aware of these sensations in their body will help them regulate their eating behavior in the future.

Holidays are associated with candy (e.g., Halloween, Easter, Thanksgiving, and Christmas). Candy should be allocated by piece, not by the bag or basket!

2. Pursue Nutritional Balance

If preventive strategies haven't been successful and a child overeats and grows fat despite all the best efforts, parents may have to pursue a strategy of weight loss. Focusing on slow but steady weight reduction has an advantage over dramatic approaches that result initially in quick weight loss, but eventually in regaining the weight. A long-range study should include a change in attitude and behavior, rather than just a change in caloric intake.

Make sure excessive sugar is removed from the family diet. Complex carbohydrates, such as fruits and vegetables, should be included, rather than non-nutritious junk food.

3. Increase Exercise

Although reducing caloric intake is essential, exercise is also an important ingredient in weight control. If fewer calories are ingested than burned, weight loss will eventually occur. The key is to establish a pattern of regular workouts.

Exercise can be planned with an individual or team approach. It can also be worked into day-to-day activities. Instead of driving a car to the grocery store, encourage walking or bike riding. Instead of taking the elevator to the third floor of a building, use the stairs.

4. Using Rewards

Many children are discouraged by the length of time it takes to see significant weight loss. Children like instant results, and they don't get them in a carefully designed weight-control program. Therefore, it may be necessary to use special rewards and compliments for day-to-day behavior rather than a final result. This may mean looking less at the scale and paying closer attention to regular exercise and good eating habits.

A corollary of the reward principle involves helping children develop a sense of self-reward. Children need to learn to establish their own goals, and allow themselves special privileges for progress, or deprivation if they fail. Numerous behavioral strategies including self-control and self-reward may be helpful.

5. Get to the Root of the Problem

There are times when the impetus for overeating comes from psychological problems. Some children overeat to punish parents. For insecure children, eating can be a way of seeking security and satisfaction not otherwise obtainable. For other children, obesity serves as an excuse to keep them from engaging in frightening or strenuous activities. Girls or boys may develop obesity as a way to avoid the trauma of dating, or to rule out participation in activities they don't like.

If significant emotional factors contribute to obesity, a vicious cycle is often established in which eating is used to deal with negative feelings. When obesity triggers guilt, social estrangement, and limited success, a professional's help may be needed to solve the problem.

6. Start Early

Good eating habits can be started when children are young. The family shouldn't eat in front of the television. Meals should be at the kitchen or dining room table. The family shouldn't have large amounts of cheap calorie snacks around that the child can free-feed on whenever desired. Healthy snacks, including fruit, should be available at special times, for example, after school. From early on, children can help with menu planning, and can be encouraged to include all the major food groups in meal preparations.

Anorexia Nervosa and Bulimia

Anorexia nervosa and bulimia are serious conditions that can damage health and, in extreme cases, cause death. Two strategies for dealing with these conditions are recommended: prevention and seeking professional help.

1. Prevent the Occurrence

Just as there are steps families can take to prevent overeating and obesity, there are ways to stem the occurrence of anorexia and bulimia. Children tend to imitate parents, and thin parents tend to have thin children. If parents are obsessed with thinness, children may have the same preoccupation. Parents who are rigid about what they eat can't avoid setting a similar pattern in children.

As much as possible, mealtimes should be pleasant and conflict-free. They shouldn't include arguments or other tense dialogue that sends people away from the table as soon as possible. There should be adequate time for eating, and children should be encouraged to eat at their own pace without dawdling.

Parents who convey a sense of understanding can help children express anger and hostility, rather than suppress it. Children should be encouraged to express negative feelings so those emotions won't convert to destructive eating habits.

2. Seek Professional Help

Because of the danger, immediate professional consultation is required for either of these problems. The signs of anorexia are often apparent. The child, usually a girl, is very thin and obsessed with thinness to the point of eating very little or overexercising.

Detecting bulimia is much more difficult. The bingeing and purging aspects of this disorder usually occur in private. Parents should look for evidence that vast amounts of food have been consumed by children in a brief period of time. Also, frequent use of the bathroom, accompanied by running water, may signal self-induced vomiting.

Chapter Six

Problems of Immaturity

Children who seem to show a delay in any aspect of development are often considered immature. Immature behavior is usually viewed as more characteristic of a younger child. Children develop unevenly, and they can be mature in one area and immature in another. Immature behaviors frustrate and embarrass parents. In this chapter, we will cover some of the typical immature behaviors, including bed wetting, misusing allowances, distractibility and inattentiveness, and manipulative crying.

Bed Wetting

Most children stop wetting the bed by the age of five. Many, however, have occasional accidents after that age, making bed wetting a frequently discussed childhood problem.

Various strategies, discussed here, have been developed to deal with bed wetting.

1. Eliminate Excessive Attention

Many children who continue wetting the bed after age five probably do it to get their parents' attention. Parents who respond by constantly reminding children of their bad habit, imposing such penalties as forbidding them anything to drink after 7:00 P.M., telling them they must go to the bathroom before going to bed, or waking them several times during the night to have them urinate are catering to the child's attention-seeking needs and may intensify the bed wetting.

A better strategy is to eliminate attention regarding the problem. Stopping the bed wetting isn't as easy as stopping thumb sucking. It requires diligence and tolerance. As a start, explain matter-of-factly to children that because of their ages, bed wetting is something for them to deal with themselves. Tell them, "You're old enough now to take care of yourself." This should be done in a pleasant, nonblaming, nonpunitive way, without giving any extra attention.

Show children, based on their ages, how to make their beds, where to put soiled linens and pajamas, and how to wash rubber or plastic sheets. Children should practice cleaning the wet bed. Then make it clear you won't explain the regimen again, nor check the bed for wetness. When children brag about having a dry bed, respond in a calm, supportive manner, showing no excessive concern. Leave this problem and resolution totally up to them.

2. Don't Overreact

Taking a child to a pediatrician solely for bed wetting may bring undue attention to the issue, embarrass the child, and promote a sense of failure. Any medical causes for the problem would likely be discovered in routine checkups. If there's concern about a possible medical cause, discuss it in the context of other medical problems.

3. Watch for Regression

Some children wet the bed because they like being treated like a baby and having others do things for them. It's particularly common for children to adopt this attitude and behavior when a new sibling is on the way or has arrived, because another sibling can be threatening to a child and produce feelings of insecurity and envy. The child's new theory is this: "Everybody seems to be excited about the new baby. Perhaps if I'm a baby, people will get excited about me, too." Reassure your children by giving them special attention, especially after there's a new baby in the house.

4. Use the Bell-and-Pad Technique

When bed wetting is resistant to less intense strategies, the bell-and-pad technique is often effective. This is a well-documented strategy using solid psychological principles. A pad is placed on the bed and attached to a bell. When a child wets, the bell goes off. The parent comes into the room, awakens the child, and has the youngster finish urinating in the toilet. Eventually, the child learns to do this alone, and an association is established between a full bladder and awakening.

Equipment for the bell-and-pad technique and other simple devices is available through medical supply stores (mail-order stores such as Sears and Montgomery Ward.) One bit of warning: This method can initially be disruptive because of the harsh sound awakening the child, but it may be a small price to pay for a dry bed.

5. Use Dry Bed Training

Dr. Nathan H. Azrin and Richard M. Foxx have developed an ingenious strategy for dealing with childhood bed wetting problems. Their procedure, called "dry bed training," is too elaborate to be appropriately explained here. Their book, *Toilet Training in Less Than a Day* (New York: Pocket Books, 1974), is available in bookstores.

6. Use a Reward System

Reward dry nights for frequent bed wetters. Lavish praise, encouragement, and perhaps stars or other symbols on a chart would be appropriate. Such incentives help children acquire self-discipline.

One way for structuring this system is to set up a program whereby a child is rewarded after a single dry night, then after two consecutive dry nights, then three. This continues until a child has been dry for a month, then is phased out.

7. Try Retention-Control Training

Some research indicates bed wetters have decreased bladder capacity and can be helped by promoting bladder expansion. Using this approach, a child is taught to increase the time between awareness of the urge to urinate and the act of urination. A child could be asked to delay urination for up to five minutes at first, then to gradually delay it as much as half an hour. Before attempting this strategy, check with a pediatrician.

A similar strategy focuses on the amount of urine. A child urinates into a measuring cup, and the amount is recorded. The child then tries to surpass the old mark during subsequent urinations. Research shows that if children are able to void over nine ounces of urine at one time, they aren't likely to be enuretic at night.

8. Train the Sphincter Muscle

Some professionals suggest nocturnal enuresis can be aided by strengthening the sphincter muscle associated with the bladder. This muscle, often called the doughnut muscle, can be strengthened if the child practices starting and stopping urination a couple of times each day. This probably won't have instantaneous results, but it can eventually reduce enuresis. Highly motivated children can be asked to stop urinating in midstream, then start and stop again every few seconds.

9. Employ Corrective Consequences

One school of thought on this issue suggests there should be a response-cost consequence for having a wet bed. Such a strategy goes beyond the natural consequences of laundering sheets and remaking the bed, to include loss of privileges or a fine.

If this strategy is used, it should be without nagging, criticism, or lecturing. Positive consequences for dry nights are usually more effective than negative consequences for wet nights. In especially difficult cases, a combined approach may be effective.

10. Try Nightly Awakening

Awakening children and taking them half-asleep to the bathroom to avoid bed wetting is not usually effective. A staggered-awakening technique is more effective. For example, children who usually wet two to three hours after going to sleep should be awakened and taken to the bathroom just before that time. If they're dry and successfully void in the toilet, parents could give a reward.

Following seven consecutive dry nights using this process, parents set the alarm for ninety minutes after bedtime. After another seven consecutive dry nights, the alarm is set for sixty minutes. Following another week of success, the alarm is set for half an hour. The procedure can then be phased out by using the alarm one night and not using it the next. After seven more dry nights, the alarm is eliminated. This strategy is particularly effective with highly motivated teenagers.

Misuse of Money and Allowances

By the time children are preschoolers, they have some understanding of money. Later, problems with money may develop when children discuss allowances and possibilities of earning cash. The common-sense approaches suggested here frequently solve most of these problems.

1. Give Allowances

Some theorists suggest parents give children a regular allowance beginning at preschool age. Children do nothing special to earn the money, and can spend it any way they want. The allowance is viewed as simply a right that comes with being in the family. It doesn't have to be a large sum. It's merely a way to start teaching children how to be responsible with money.

2. Put Them to Work

In addition to daily chores, older children should be given the opportunity of doing extra jobs around the house. These bonus jobs may include mowing the lawn, washing the car, shoveling snow, or painting a room. Children should be paid a reasonable amount for doing the work.

3. Assign Regular Chores

One of the more controversial topics among disciplinarians is whether to compensate for regular chores. Behaviorists advocate giving children money for completing chores. They don't necessarily recommend children continue to be paid for doing the chores until they reach adulthood; however, to get a child started doing regular chores, the use of money as a reward is encouraged. Other disciplinarians abhor the use of money as a reward for chores normally expected of a child. Perhaps parents would do well to use a combination approach, compensating children for special or unusual chores, but not for routine chores expected of them.

4. Establish Spending Rules

Many disciplinarians suggest parents allow children to use money as they choose, as long as it's not for illicit purposes. In this case, the children shouldn't be forced to commit a certain percentage of their earnings to savings. Rather, they should be permitted to make financial mistakes so they can learn to avoid them when they're older.

5. Make Loans

Parents aren't banks, and shouldn't loan money to a child. It's generally not a good idea to get into financial deals with children. If children want to buy something, it's up to them to figure out how to pay for it. There are times, however, when parents may want to help finance a large item. Their help should be treated as a gift, not a loan. In general, parents shouldn't purchase a large item for an older child without the youngster contributing a down payment. Even though older children may have significant musical ability, for example, parents shouldn't try to buy thousands of dollars' worth of electronic organs, synthesizers, speakers, and amplifiers without the children pitching in on the cost.

6. Resist Peer Pressure

By the time children reach pre-adolescence, they may complain that "everybody" gets more allowance than they do. They may say they can't buy the things everybody else has, or that they don't have fashionable clothes others are wearing. Parents should anticipate such arguments and remind themselves and their children the allowance they agreed on is fair. If children really want new or better possessions, they should find a way to earn the extra money.

7. Suspend Allowances and Institute Fines

Fining children or suspending their allowances is a possible penalty. On the other hand, some authorities suggest the allowance is a right that shouldn't be suspended, and once money is earned, it shouldn't be taken away. We recommend selecting the method that best suits a particular family, and then using it with absolute consistency.

8. Use the Developmental Approach

In his book *Keeping Parents out of Trouble*, Dr. Dan Kiley outlines a four-stage process for teaching children the value of money ([New York: Warner Books, 1981], 253–257]). The first stage covers ages two to four. During this stage, Dr. Kiley suggests using tokens to help explain the relationship between working and enjoying the fruits of one's labor.

When a task is completed, children are rewarded. Dr. Kiley also suggests when children ask for a treat they should have to perform a concrete task to earn it. Any other treat is labeled "special," because it doesn't have to be earned.

The second stage in Kiley's program occurs between ages five and eight. During this time, a chore chart or checklist is used. Every time a responsible action is completed, a check is placed in the appropriate box, and children are then rewarded at least weekly. At this stage, children have to wait at least a few days between the time the work is completed and the time they get rewarded.

In the third stage, for ages nine to twelve, children are asked to do routine tasks without compensation, but are given an allowance so they have spending money. Fines can be used if regular jobs aren't handled well.

Kiley's fourth stage covers ages thirteen and up. The children are told that from then on, their allowance is suspended, and they'll have to earn the money they need, perhaps by doing extra or occasional jobs around the house. They're also encouraged to talk to friends, neighbors, and relatives about availability for work, and told that at least 20 percent of all earnings must be saved.

Contrary to most disciplinarians, Dr. Kiley favors personal loans to children in this age bracket. His reasoning is that this stage of development should facilitate a child's entry into the real financial world.

9. Take Away Lunch Money

Many children, especially adolescents, often skip lunches and use their lunch money for cigarettes, drugs, alcohol, or junk food. In schools where lunch tickets are used, some children sell them at a discount to fellow students, and use the money for other things. A simple solution to this problem is to deprive them of lunch money, and leave them the choice of packing their own lunch or not eating at all until they can guarantee they'll use the money responsibly.

10. Try a Response Cost

Some children are not necessarily invested in earning money, because it seems like too much work. However, they often don't want to lose any money that has been given to them. In this respect, another strategy that is almost the opposite of earning money is to give them a set amount of money each week. This money is sort of a retainer fee. It can be decreased or taken away for not completing the daily tasks and chores that are expected. In this respect, the children have not earned the money and you are not taking away a reward that they have been given; rather, you are reversing the strategy of getting them to comply with household tasks and chores. Again, this works best when children are not necessarily invested in earning money but certainly do not want any of their money taken away.

Overly Active, Distractible, and Inattentive Behavior

Young children are often expected to be reckless, inattentive, and distractible. As they get older, however, they should become more mature and self-controlled. They should pay attention better, be more reflective and less impulsive, and solve problems more effectively. Yet, this doesn't always happen.

When inattentiveness and distractibility occur, they raise havoc at home and at school. Also, it's difficult for children with these traits to learn effectively. Children diagnosed as hyperactive and having the attention deficit associated with that disorder aren't the subject here. We are discussing the youngsters who (because of anxiety, disorganization, and temperament) are reckless, expansive, and overactive. Thirteen possible strategies are offered as a means of correcting these problems.

1. Establish a Structured Environment

Children in general, and especially those who suffer from immature behaviors, need clear limits. They should be told what's expected of them and the consequences of not meeting those expectations. Expectations should be stated verbally and in writing. Also, be consistent and predictable in setting expectations and in administering the consequences.

2. Model the Behavior

Impulsive, expansive, and restless children often have parents or older siblings who act similarly. If parents overreact and make careless decisions without thinking them through, they set the stage for similar behavior from their offspring. If children observe their parents being reflective and purposeful, they'll likely do the same. Statements like, "First I have to finish this job, then I'll be able to sit down and relax," "Let's stop and think. What's the best way to figure this out?" or "This isn't working, so let's set aside some time and try to figure it out," serve as critical models in fostering similar behavior in their children.

3. Use Charts and Contracts

Immature children benefit from visible feedback. Charts and contracts are specific strategies for giving children feedback immediately after the desired behavior occurs. Also, use checks, stars, tokens, or chips as symbolic rewards that can be cashed in for privileges, treats, or toys. Some parents walk around with poker chips in their pockets, giving them to children whenever they engage in proper behavior. Different colored chips should be used for each child to avoid confusion and theft.

Another strategy is to reward children for sticking to a task for a minimum amount of time. For example, waking hours at home can be broken into fifteen-minute segments. If on-task behavior occurs during a specific interval and no significant distractions occur, children are rewarded.

4. Repeat Directions

Many distractible and inattentive children don't listen to or remember what parents say to them. It helps to ask children to repeat directions after they've been given, then repeat them again about ten minutes later. This induced recall process assures parents that their instructions are received and remembered. If children show that they can remember directions without repetition, then repetition isn't needed. But if a child's recall slips, instructions should be repeated until learned.

5. Rewarding Appropriate Behavior

Parents can encourage on-task behavior by rewarding it with warm feedback. This verbal-reward approach can be used for a variety of immature behaviors. Whenever a child shows reflection or consideration of consequences, mention the specifics of the good behavior and congratulate the youngster. Conversely, use mild negative consequences—such as fines or brief time in isolation—for inattentive or impulsive behavior.

6. Encourage Self-Talk

To help children become more mature and attentive, encourage appropriate self-talk. When children engage in inattentive activity, ask them to rethink their approach to the situation by saying to themselves aloud, "Stop, look, and think!" If parents encourage children to talk purposefully out loud, there's a good chance they will eventually begin to transfer this overt instruction to covert control, reducing their distractible behavior.

Another verbal approach is to encourage children to constantly question themselves, urging such queries as "What am I supposed to be doing?" or "How am I supposed to do it?" Children also need to internalize verbal rewards. They need to be able to say to themselves, "Nice job. That was great! You did it all yourself!"

Use of purposeful self-talk may include self-rewards. Children can be taught to set up their own reward systems. They might learn to say, "First, I'll finish this math problem, then I'll be able to watch TV." The key ingredient in enhancing self-talk is learning to delay gratification. Children want things right now. They don't like to wait. Appropriate self-talk could include such statements as, "I can wait my turn" or "Nothing horrible is going to happen if I'm not first in line" or "It won't hurt me if I have to watch a different TV show for now."

7. Model Self-Talk

Parents of immature children often feel embarrassed by their offspring's behavior. They think other people are staring at them disapprovingly because their children aren't well mannered.

Remind yourself that you don't need unconditional approval of other adults, and as long as you're following strategies to help children overcome problems, nothing more can be expected. Harsh feedback frequently comes from relatives who insist parents aren't being firm enough with immature children. Don't take such criticism too seriously.

8. Employ Cognitive Problem Solving

Drs. Myrna Shure and George Spivack have developed a problem-solving strategy to help children become more reflective and less impulsive (*Problem Solving Techniques in Child Rearing* [San Francisco: Jossey-Bass, 1978], chap. 1). Their strategy, which can be taught even to preschoolers, is threefold.

After a specific and usually interpersonal problem has been identified, children are asked to enumerate as many alternative solutions as possible. In the first stage, children are told not to make evaluations of solutions, but to merely think about alternatives, feasible or not. Parents can then suggest additional solutions as necessary.

The second step is to discuss probable consequences, good and bad, of each solution. Considerations should include feelings of other people involved, as well as the children's.

The third stage is to evaluate each solution based on its consequences and determine whether it's a good or bad idea.

Children won't acquire the problem-solving strategy overnight. It'll take many repetitions. However, the process of doing it usually discourages impulsivity and encourages reflection.

The problem-solving strategy can also be used in informal discussions at home involving other people. For example, at the dinner table, a family could use this approach in deciding possible solutions to problems that don't involve the child. The key is helping children generate solutions and evaluate consequences.

In a nutshell, this strategy reflects a common-sense approach: The more solutions people have to a problem, the better they'll be able to solve it. Generally speaking, adolescents who can enumerate a large number of solutions to a problem are better adjusted than those who can list only a few solutions.

9. Use a Timer

For some children, a timer can play a valuable role. Place the timer on a desk while children are working on school projects. Its nearly inaudible ticking sometimes serves as a subtle and mysterious force that keeps the children on task. Why this happens isn't clear, and not all children respond to this tactic. Many, however, seem to focus more effectively on their work when a timer is running nearby.

10. Try Bibliotherapy

The local librarian can help identify books on problem-solving that can help children learn to overcome impulsive actions. Here are a few books we like.

For younger children:

Cleary, Beverly B. *Henry and the Clubhouse.* West Caldwell, N.J.: William Morrow, 1962.

Lexau, Joan M. *Benjie on His Own.* New York: Dial Press, 1970.

Nadeau, Kathleen G., and Ellen B. Dixon. *Learning to Slow Down and Pay Attention.* Annandale, Va.: Chesapeake Psychological Publications, 1993.

For older children:

Gantos, Jack. *Joey Pigza Swallowed the Key.* New York: HarperTrophy, 1998.

Janover, Caroline. *Zipper: The Kid with ADHD.* Bethesda, Md.: Woodbine House, 1997.

11. Reduce Anxiety and Stress

Some children become inattentive or distracted because of high anxiety levels. They feel insecure, scared, and nervous, and consequently have difficulty paying attention.

Studies have shown a little anxiety facilitates performance, but high levels impair it. It a child's inattentiveness appears to be rooted in anxiety, try removing sources of stress and increase coping strategies to improve his or her self-concept.

12. Eliminate Physical Discomfort

Children's attention spans vary considerably, depending on their physical comfort. Hungry or tired children tend to be restless and inattentive. When they have to go to the bathroom, they're unable to concentrate well on other activities. Children with subtle visual or hearing problems also can have difficulty with attentiveness. Some children may require professional consultation, but others may be helped at home.

Timing is critical when giving children directions. It's wise not to give them instructions or let them do homework just before meals, while they're waiting to go to the bathroom, or when they're tired.

13. Act It Out

Good actors and actresses can keep an audience spellbound even when the content of their script isn't interesting. They hold their audience by words as well as actions, fluctuating the rate, tone, and inflection of speech, and by using dramatic gestures.

These strategies can be used to capture the attention of distractible children. In addition, parents can make physical contact with children, putting a hand on their shoulders or heads. With some highly inattentive youngsters, it may be necessary to actually hold their heads.

Manipulative Crying

This section is concerned with children who use frequent crying as a way of making adults feel guilty, or as a way of exerting power.

A number of strategies can help parents deal with children who use crying as a means of manipulation.

1. Determine the Underlying Causes

First, it's important to know the difference between chronic manipulative crying and legitimate tears. The key is knowing when tears reflect hurt and deserve sympathy, and when they're being used as weapons and require a different strategy. Responding to children's feelings without yielding to a request or protest is a good strategy for determining whether tears are genuine. If empathic response calms a child, it's likely the tears are authentic. But if empathy has no calming effect, the tears are likely manipulative, and probably won't stop until the child's objective is reached.

2. Shift the Blame

Manipulative criers often explain an outburst by saying someone has hurt them, thereby shifting blame and making a pitch for pity. To verify this, parents can have children restate what happened, putting it in the first person. For example, instead of saying, "Jimmy made fun of me," the child should restate what he said in this way: "I'm really angry and upset because Jimmy called me a slowpoke." Manipulative criers often portray themselves as victims and scapegoats. It's important, therefore, to get them to assume responsibility for what happened and to admit their roles in a conflict.

3. Use Active Ignoring

Because the goal of manipulative crying is getting attention, it can be thwarted by ignoring it. Active ignoring works eventually but requires patience and persistence and means giving children no visual, verbal, or other attention of any kind.

4. Give Selective Attention

In conjunction with active ignoring, provide the child with lots of attention for not crying. If she handles a touchy situation without a crying spell, reward her.

In addition, implement a structured reward program. "Pete, from now on we're going to divide every day into sixteen periods. For each hour you don't cry, you'll get a token. You can exchange tokens at the end of the day for certain privileges. But remember, if you cry even once during an hour period, you won't receive a token." Supplement tokens with generous compliments and social approval.

5. Ask the Child to Cry Louder and Longer

This is a paradoxical strategy that can be used when a parent is convinced the crying is not in response to a legitimate need. Coach the child to cry louder or longer in an effort to eliminate the manipulation, and hence, the crying. "I've heard you do better than that" or "Is that the loudest you can cry?" may be ideas for the paradox.

6. Change the Subject

Parents can try any strategy to divert attention from manipulative criers. For example, during a crying bout, say, "Look, it's sunny outside!" or "Oh my gosh, I forgot to throw this box in the garbage."

7. Try the Prevention Chair

Tell manipulative criers, "Whenever you feel you have to cry, I want you to come and sit on this chair. There will always be a box of tissues there. When you sit on the chair, the whole family will know you want to be left alone until your tears have stopped. After you're done crying, we can talk about what happened." The message is clear: Immature, crybaby behavior won't be tolerated. When the child chooses to behave more maturely, parents will listen. Until then, the youngster has a designated place to cry without the involvement of others.

8. Plan a Family Discussion

A manipulative crier causes considerable frustration and distress. Try discussing the problem openly at a family meeting with the crybaby present. Other children in the family should have a chance to offer comments. Then the whole family can establish a plan to help the crybaby become more mature and deal more effectively with problems.

9. Read a Book

As is the case with many interpersonal problems, children who cry for attention can be helped by identifying with heroes who overcome similar problems in stories. A librarian can be helpful in locating such books.

In the next chapter we'll deal with school-related problems, including motivation and truancy. Successfully solving school challenges also leads to enhanced self-concept.

Chapter Seven

School-Related Problems

Parents view education as important because it can prepare children to deal with the world and be successful in life. But many children see education as boring, irrelevant, and unpleasant. Lack of motivation, truancy, and other problems can lead to significant under-achievement, which is often accompanied by irresponsible and imma-ture behavior. In addition, anxiety about performance in the classroom can pose problems.

School-related conflicts pose significant problems for many fami-lies. This chapter deals with three of these problems: balking at going to school, underachievement, and truancy.

Balking at Going to School

Especially in the early years, children sometimes are reluctant to go to school. They may complain of various aches and pains. They may even cry or become frantic. This can be distressing for parents, who let the child stay home. The more this behavior is allowed, the higher the likelihood of recurrence, perhaps with even greater intensity. In some severe cases, it becomes virtually impossible to send children to school. Ten strategies have proved effective in easing and eliminating the problem.

1. Prepare for Separation

Most children don't have an actual school phobia. What they expe-rience is discomfort at being separated from their parents. It isn't fear of school that bothers them, but anxiety about being alone in an unfamiliar setting.

Parents can help children prepare for school by having them spend time away from home, perhaps in the home of a relative, friend, or baby-sitter. Intermittent experiences in preschool or daycare settings also can be helpful. If the separation might be more difficult for the parents than the child, the parent needs to prepare for separation first and set a calm, unemotional example for the children.

2. Be Empathic but Firm

When children complain of aches and pains in the morning, let them know you understand. At the same time, emphasize the importance of going to school. Unless children are vomiting or have a fever, they should not miss classes. Send the children off or take them to school, but make the separation firm and clean. Lingering, looking back, or other forms of hesitation only reinforce refusal behavior.

3. Suspect Other Causes

Sometimes children begin balking after experiencing teasing or other forms of cruelty from classmates. These children feel so uncomfortable about going to school they put up every objection possible. Regardless of the situation, it's important for them to go. If the problem persists, however, get to the bottom of it. If you determine that provocative behavior is occurring at school, talk to school personnel about it. Also, you can help your child learn to cope with the cruel taunting of others.

4. Check Out the Teacher

When children go to school, they find a whole new world. Often their teachers have different rules. Some teachers can't give much individual attention because of large numbers of children in the classroom. At home, rules may be relaxed and flexible; at school, they tend to be more rigid.

Many children have problems dealing with change. Sometimes they even have an inept teacher. There are poorly qualified people in every profession, and teaching is no exception. Some teachers are nonempathic, harsh, cruel, or ridiculing and often harmful to vulnerable children.

If you determine your children's problems are because of a teacher's behavior, discuss the matter with the school administrators and assertively pursue alternative solutions. Also, tell children that a teacher's apparent dislike for them doesn't make them less important or lovable.

5. Practice Positive Self-Talk

Children who experience discomfort going to school may begin a phobic process on Sunday afternoon or evening. When that happens, encourage children to talk realistically and logically to themselves. They can say, "Going to school requires a lot of courage, but I can do it." Or "I know it's sometimes hard to go to school, but I can be brave and do hard things." Before children go to bed, tell them gently that they must go to school whether they like it or not, and reassure them that it isn't such a terrible experience.

6. Try a Mental Exercise

Another way to desensitize children is to have them list the steps involved in getting ready for school. Starting the night before, this can include doing homework, getting books ready, and selecting clothes. The next morning, have them continue listing the steps including dressing, eating breakfast, going to the bus, riding to school, and walking into class. This mental exercise performed in a calm, disciplined way may help reduce fears.

7. Seek Professional Help

When school refusal gets to the point where there's hysterical crying, violent tantrums, and absolute refusal to enter the building, it's time for professional consultation. The professional usually meets with the child in psychotherapy and establishes a formal treatment plan to get them back into school. The plan may use some gradual exposure components. On the other hand, it may involve a very firm application of a common rule: children not vomiting or without a fever must be in school.

8. Reward Bravery

In addition to other strategies, reward children who go to school and don't complain of any physical discomfort. In this case, it is important to reward two different aspects of the school refusal pattern. First, give children an opportunity to earn a reward for voicing no physical complaints before going to school. Second, reward them for expressing no physical complaints once in school.

9. Deal with True Sickness

If a child is ill—perhaps showing symptoms of vomiting or a fever—don't reward her in any way. Give minimal attention. She should stay in bed and not be able to watch TV. Furthermore, no games or any pleasurable activity whatsoever should be engaged in during school hours. As soon as symptoms subside, the youngster should return to school.

10. Employ Bibliotherapy

A number of children's books contain stories of how heroes in the story learn to conquer their fears. One example is *I'd Rather Stay Home* by Carol Barkin and Elizabeth James (Milwaukee: Raintree Editions; Chicago: Children's Press, 1978). Your librarian or the internet are good sources as well. Some stories deal with discomfort about school, either directly or indirectly. As with other problems, reading stories about children who cope with fears can be influential in helping the child cope with fears.

11. Prearrange a Planned Activity

One strategy that is often beneficial in helping children go to school is to discuss with them a planned activity they will do as soon as they get there. Prearrange the activity with the teacher and include tasks like checking in other students, participating in getting something ready for the rest of the students like handing out worksheets, or some other activity that includes the teacher. It may include an activity with another student, which could be prearranged with the other student's parents. Perhaps the child would meet another student at a particular place outside of the school building and walk in hand-in-hand or meet another student at a particular place and exchange a dessert that they will eat at lunch or have some kind of conversation about the school day. Sometimes having a planned activity to get the school day rolling helps get reluctant students to go to school.

Underachievement and Poor Study Habits

Parents place great importance on children's education, but this attitude can be carried too far. Some parents believe children should do homework and do it very well—to a point of creating problems.

Homework creates conflict in many families. Here are strategies for creating a pleasant, stimulating, curious, and intellectual atmosphere at home through positive encouragement, rather than through negative or corrective means.

1. Use Examples, Not Lectures

Children hear plenty of lectures about learning while they're in school. Another one at home is likely to create boredom and disinterest. You can motivate children to study and learn by setting a good example, by showing curiosity and interest in the world around you, or by subscribing to newspapers and magazines and discussing their topics.

By listening to your discussions, children can learn to form opinions and gather information. You can also show an interest in learning by taking courses and setting the example of doing homework, or by playing educational games with your children to stimulate interest. In addition to reading and discussing current publications, have good reference books at home, such as a dictionary and a set of encyclopedias. By setting appropriate examples, you can gently nudge a child into an enthusiasm for learning. But relentlessly pushing children can squelch curiosity and diminish their desire to learn.

2. Let the Schools Do Their Work

How involved should parents become in their child's schoolwork? Many disciplinarians argue that parents shouldn't take part at all in their children's formal schooling, because specialists are paid to do that job. Some experts recommend parents avoid monitoring homework. Parents' only participation in a child's formal schooling, they say, should come when the child requests help with specific assignments. Other experts advocate a noncommittal response with no rewards or penalties related to schoolwork. When children don't know answers to problems, parents help them out but don't reveal what the answers are. These hard-nosed disciplinarians maintain this attitude even when a child is about to flunk or drop out of school. This approach is excessive and counterproductive. Some involvement is necessary. The question is how much. We suggest being reasonable.

3. Be Reasonable

Parents can get caught up in the irrational belief that if their children don't receive straight As or aren't headed for college, they'll be failures. Not all children are destined for college and not all children need formal education to be successful. In fact, many university graduates are less successful than those who didn't graduate. Parents need to remind themselves they're not failures if their child doesn't earn diplomas or degrees beyond high school.

4. Praise Your Children

Children who don't receive enough attention at home find disruptive ways of demanding it at school. Also, youngsters whose parents expect As and Bs all the time may only get attention when they bring home low grades or bad-conduct reports. Because these children find it difficult to earn the grades their parents expect, they seek attention through academic underachievement.

Some children seek attention by being the class clown. The more they disrupt the classroom, the more classmates laugh and pay attention to them. For certain unhappy, insecure children, this clowning brings rewards.

The solution doesn't lie in the area of academic assistance. Instead, parents should praise children in the presence of peers for positive and cooperative work. Try inviting one of your child's friends to go along on an outing, making sure your child receives generous verbal praise for good behavior during that time. Some ingenious parents set up neighborhood projects in which their child emerges as a leader or hero. Good behavior should be followed by praise, preferably in the presence of peers. Another strategy is to suggest a teacher arrange for similar kinds of rewards for the child at school. This technique helps satisfy a child's needs for attention, and reduces negative behavior.

5. Be Realistic

Socially mobile parents, such as the country club set and aspiring executives, are targets for blackmail and manipulation with respect to children's grades and conduct. This happens when these parents convey an overwhelming need for perfection. To impress high-achieving friends, they often expect too much from their children.

Children have ample ammunition for retaliating against parents who seem more concerned about what their friends think than about them. Such parents need to change their attitudes and beliefs. Just because children are disruptive at school doesn't mean they'll be destitute or social outcasts someday.

It's rewarding to have high-achieving, well-mannered children. But it's not always possible. Parents need to rechannel anxiety and dissatisfaction about children's imperfections rather than give them more power and ammunition for misbehavior.

6. Arrange for Feedback

Some disciplinarians advocate close communication between school officials and parents, with consequences at home based on performance at school. Consequences based on quarterly re-port-card grades usually have no impact because there's too much time between the behavior and the consequence. Yet, despite their busy schedules, many teachers will provide daily or weekly feedback to parents.

A simple feedback sheet might list the day's classes and a grading system, such as ABCDF or 54321. In each class, the teacher circles a grade for each day or week, and signs or initials the form. Rewards and consequences are given depending on predetermined criteria. For example, for every daily grade above a C, a child might receive an extra half-hour of free time or an allowance bonus. But for each grade below C, the child might be grounded a half-hour or assigned extra chores. In using this approach, the par-

Daily Report Card

Student _____ Date _____

Class	Unaccept-able	Poor	Fair	Good	Great
English	1	2	3	4	5
Science	1	2	3	4	5
Math	1	2	3	4	5
Social Studies	1	2	3	4	5
Reading	1	2	3	4	5
Spelling	1	2	3	4	5
Art/Music	1	2	3	4	5

ent should deal matter-of-factly, avoiding criticism, lecturing, and preaching. If conduct rather than grades is a child's problem, a similar form can be designed using behavioral ratings.

7. Avoid Double Jeopardy
If children are punished at school for breaking rules, don't punish them again at home for the same crime.

8. Enlist the Teacher's Help

As much as possible, children who aren't performing well in a class should be responsible for enlisting a teacher's assistance, at least initially. This action can nudge them into maturity by enhancing a sense of responsibility.

Many teachers feel responsible for academic underachievement in their classrooms. When they're approached directly by a student who genuinely and earnestly professes an interest in turning the situation around, most teachers respond positively. If a teacher refuses to help, parents should immediately get involved and set up a meeting.

9. Enforce Study Sessions

Parents can initiate learning sessions by setting up specific study time at home, such as quiet periods after school and on weekends. During that time, children are required to do assigned homework or read other materials quietly. They can also be urged to consult with parents about the work they are doing.

Scheduling home study sessions helps children realize learning can occur anywhere and anytime, and isn't restricted to school. As a rule, a half-hour is a good length of quiet time for grade-school children, forty-five minutes for junior high students, and an hour to an hour and a half for high schoolers.

10. Foster the Right Perspective

The joy and excitement of early learning experiences (for example, *Sesame Street, The Electric Company, Mr. Rogers, Barney and Friends,* and other children's programming) can lead some children to expect that learning will always be fun, never boring. Children who harbor this illogical belief need assistance in developing a more realistic attitude toward studies.

Although learning isn't always fun and exciting, it can be made more interesting. This responsibility shouldn't fall on the teacher alone. Parents and children should share it. One way is to play educational games, such as Scrabble, Cribbage, Lotto, or Twenty Questions. These games help a child to learn while having fun.

11. Teach Study Skills

Many parents mistakenly assume children learn how to study in school. Many teachers, however, don't teach such basic study techniques as efficient reading, note taking, and test preparation. Starting in the elementary grades, youngsters need to acquire these skills. They need to learn that reading for knowledge isn't the same as reading for pleasure. Children also can benefit from memory tricks and study strategies outlined in books on the subject such as *The Memory Book,* by Jerry Lucas and Harry Lorayne (New York: Ballantine Books, 1986).

If you think you can't teach these skills to your children, consider hiring a tutor. The boredom and anguish of learning can often be reduced through improved study habits. Most people—children included—can learn large amounts of material rapidly if they use a systematic approach. Children should be taught effective self-talk, self-rewards, and self-punishment. They need to know that if they work diligently for half an hour, they can reward themselves, for example, by watching a TV show.

Also, they can set up a mild punishment system for themselves if they daydream frequently or are easily distracted from studying. Snapping a rubber band on the wrist is one harmless method that serves as a reminder of the task at hand.

Children can establish their own remedies for study distractions. For example, they might set a rule that if anyone phones while they're doing homework, the caller will be told to call again later. They also might keep the radio or TV turned off, and ask family members to keep quiet.

12. Assess Your Parents' Attitudes

Parental attitudes are a critical variable in a child's school-related behavior. Parents communicate expectations regarding school. Some establish high standards for their children, and expect adherence. Others expect less than youngsters are capable of delivering, which can cause an immature and dependent academic style.

Parents who are uninvolved in their children's schoolwork imply learning isn't important. Their children follow suit, placing no value on study efforts. Other parents don't establish self-discipline as a goal for their children. Thus, their children lack a disciplined approach to schoolwork. Self-discipline doesn't develop in isolated areas of a child's life. It usually is evident in most dimensions or not at all. If self-discipline isn't expected in and outside the home, it won't develop in school.

Parental attitudes can contribute to children's underachievement. Therefore, parents should carefully assess their attitudes, and make necessary changes. Children with low esteem aren't often motivated to succeed, so they set unrealistic goals for themselves. Raising self-esteem in all areas helps a child become a better achiever. Achieving doesn't necessarily mean getting all As. It means performing at a level commensurate with one's ability.

13. Get Involved in School

In some school districts, there are attitudes of indifference toward learning and academic achievement. Such attitudes are reflected by teachers, the administration, and, the school board. Parents should try changing these attitudes by working through the school board and parent-teacher associations.

Administrators respond to groups of parents who aren't trying to contradict or undermine them but want to provide the best educational atmosphere for their children. In many school districts, parental interest and involvement have led to positive changes.

14. Establish a Positive Mind-Set

Some children have defeatist attitudes about learning. They become so discouraged they believe nothing positive or satisfying can occur in school. Much work with fantasy and imagery, which has proved successful in athletic performance, also can be applied to academic achievement.

First, children need to establish models they want to emulate. Those models can be great athletes, scientists, thinkers, writers, or older students in the same school. Whoever the models are, it's important to study them and find out what made them high achievers.

Second, children must paint mental images of themselves in successful roles. For example, they could imagine they're taking a test and doing well on it, or receiving an award for outstanding work.

Third, they need to eradicate all negative thoughts, such as "I can't get it," "Nothing comes easily for me," or "I might just as well give up." Children should replace those thoughts with more positive ones like "If I keep trying, I'll get it," or "Even though it's tough, I'm not going to give up. If I keep trying, I'll master it."

Finally, children need to establish a reward system, giving themselves positive feedback following small achievements. This power of positive thinking may be the best first step toward improved academic achievement.

15. Write an Autobiography

To obtain clues regarding patterns of underachievement, ask children to write their autobiographies. Reading them may give clues about family factors, poor goals, poor self-esteem, and learning problems. Academic underachievement doesn't occur without reasons, and identifying them is critical.

16. Offer Choices

To minimize resistance to homework, give children the choice of doing it before or after dinner. The choice isn't whether or not to do homework, but whether to do it at one particular time or another. The forced-choice method gives children a sense of control, and may allow time for a favorite activity or television program as a reward.

17. Start Homework at School

Encourage children to begin homework assignments in class, if possible, or during study periods. If they start homework at school, follow-through at home is much easier. Many children waste time near the end of classes when teachers allow them to do homework. Time is also wasted in study halls. If children begin homework at school, they can complete it more easily at home.

18. Teach Them to Manage Their Time

As children grow and develop, it can be difficult for them to manage their time for homework and their time for other activities. As adults, we often expect children to pick up this skill on their own, but it is best to teach them how to manage their time. This can be done in the form of graphs or a schedule. Ultimately, the idea is to help students recognize that they need a certain amount of time to complete tasks. As part of the instruction, encourage them to be realistic about the amount of time needed to perform a task and to plan for extra time. It is more beneficial to have planned too much time to complete a task than it is to plan too little time. The concept of time management can be taught in different forms at a relatively early age. While the complications of activities and homework certainly get more involved as the child develops, the basic concepts of planning and organization of time can be taught even in elementary school.

Truancy

A lackadaisical attitude toward school is increasingly prevalent in our culture. Schools and parents have become more permissive. Growing numbers of children are dropping out of school by age sixteen. Many junior and senior high school students skip classes they don't like. Some may take time out from a class to party and get "high."

Truancy is a form of "copping out," and evidence of irresponsible behavior that should be nipped in the bud. Truancy often leads to early departure from school, which can result in a poor employment record. Children should learn at an early age that when the going gets tough, there are options other than quitting. Parents encountering this problem may need to try a number of the strategies presented here.

1. Reject the "Everybody Does It" Argument

When adolescents want to justify irresponsible behavior, they often use the excuse that "everybody does it." Other students may be skipping school, but "everybody" isn't. Tell your child that even if others in the class are behaving irresponsibly, it's no cause for her to do so. You might say, for instance, "I really don't care about everybody else. I care about you. Why are you doing it?" This tactic can help parents find out the real reasons for children's truancy. Perhaps the youngster is bored. Perhaps she is experiencing undue pressure from peers. Perhaps she is failing in school and can't face it. Once the real reason is determined, it'll be easier to find a solution.

2. Play Detective

Truants are often clever at covering up their actions. They may go to classes where attendance is taken, but skip all others. In those circumstances talk with the teachers of classes being skipped, so special arrangements can be made for taking attendance records. Frequent calls to the school also can help to determine whether a child is there or not.

If children "play hooky" from school, there must be some punitive consequences. Punishment should consist primarily of loss of privileges or extra work details. An immature, irresponsible truant is clearly not entitled to privileges.

3. Seek Psychological Evaluation

Many truants experience failure in the classroom because they have subtle learning problems that haven't been identified and may have escaped the scrutiny of teachers. In these cases, consultation with a clinical or school psychologist may be necessary.

4. Don't Ask the Question if You Know the Answer

Parents often know about their child's truant behavior from other sources. Yet, when the child arrives at home, they ask, "Well, how did school go today?" These questions invite the child to step into a trap and usually result in increased hostility, anger, and bitterness. Confrontations with truant children should be direct: "Why did you skip classes today?"

5. Be a Good Role Model

Parents who call in sick because they don't feel like going to work may have children who're likely to skip school. In these cases, children learn to think it's not important to be responsible.

6. Use Preventive Strategies

Parental attitudes toward school clearly influence children's behavior. Parents who didn't complete high school, for example, may subconsciously communicate the message that education isn't important. To compensate for this, they should discourage truancy, and openly and deliberately talk to their children about the importance of staying in school.

Similarly, children who have academic difficulties and are held back in school for a year or more may be embarrassed to have younger classmates. Children should never be held back more than once, because they become more mature than others in the class, and may experience feelings of rejection or isolation.

Some children, especially shy ones, become truant because they fear violence, drug dealing, and blackmailing in their schools. They're afraid of discussing their fears and, instead, develop excuses. To help overcome such fears, an honest, candid relationship with parents is especially important. Parents who suspect there are undiscussed problems need to offer support, and try to discover the root of the problem. Only then can they determine the next step to take.

7. Use a Reward System

Many children are encouraged to attend school regularly if they earn rewards for such behavior. For example, a child may be allowed to have driving privileges or an allowance based on regular school attendance. Penalties might be imposed for unexcused absences. In school districts where truancy is pervasive, parents should encourage the PTA to recommend that the school set up incentive programs for children with good attendance records.

Truancy is difficult to eliminate with a single attempt. If students skip school as much as ten to twelve days a month, they should be asked to cut the rate in half for the next month. If this request is met, a privilege or reward can be given. Then the reward at the end of the next month should be contingent on cutting the truancy rate another 50 percent, or back to three days or fewer.

8. Use Bibliotherapy

There are some books with stories about children skipping school. These could be beneficial because they teach that problems aren't solved by running away from them. Also, they can instruct children that school has valuable benefits. We suggest these books for young truants.

Parsons, Virginia. *Pinocchio Plays Truant: Based on the Story by Carlo Collodi.* New York: McGraw Hill, 1979.

Szekeres, Cyndy. *Jumper Goes to School.* New York: Simon & Schuster, 1969.

9. Determine the Cause

It may be possible to detect patterns of truancy. For example, it may occur on days when there are tests or a gym class, or it may happen on particular days of the week. Whatever the pattern, determine what's causing your child to want to avoid school at certain times so the problem can be corrected.

10. Involve the School

Talk to the school principal or a counselor, and arrange for discussion groups made up of other students who share the same problem. These groups can discuss ways of reducing their absenteeism, and try to solve the problems that tempt them to skip classes. In involving school officials, suggest that teachers require students to make up the work missed during absences. Some teachers may resent this imposition, but parents need to work carefully and tactfully through the administration to alleviate the problem.

Ask school authorities to individualize a child's curriculum so it's less frustrating and more relevant to the child's abilities. Truant children could be given some responsible school jobs that mandate attendance, such as athletic trainer, theater stagehand, cafeteria worker, or hall monitor.

11. Consider Withdrawal

In rare cases, a student may simply not be ready for school. Perhaps the emotional consequences of a learning disability have become so devastating that the child can no longer face failure. Perhaps relentless influences of a delinquent peer group have become too much to cope with. Also, some children are too confused and immature to handle the responsibility of high school. However, if children drop out of school, they should return after working through and solving their problems.

12. Try Alternative Schools

Although this is not the first option most parents like to consider, alternative school situations may be the answer if the truancy and attendance difficulties become excessive. Most school districts offer some alternative school options, and oftentimes these schools have a different format for the school day. At some schools, the students only go to class when class is scheduled, while others have different kinds of attendance policies and scheduling classes for longer periods and allow students to get credit for a work situation. When the goal is to get your adolescent to attend school regularly and graduate from high school, sometimes an alternative educational situation is a reasonable way to go.

Beyond Discipline

In this book, we have focused on nonviolent strategies for dealing with child discipline problems. As mentioned in the Introduction, behavior management is the key to peaceful parenting, but it should be part of a holistic approach to rearing children that emphasizes prevention, communication, relationship building, and a peaceful home environment.

As with discipline strategies, the overall concept of rearing peaceful children will emerge largely out of the creativity and networking of family members. In other words, you will find methods that fit your particular situation. But to help you get started, here are some general ways to rear peaceful children.

1. Handle with Care

Peaceful parenting means no abuse of any kind. Spanking is out and so is yelling, grabbing, threatening, name calling, and the like. Hugs, nurturing touch, and calm reasoning are in. Be firm, but gentle. Use tender physical contact and a normal tone of voice to influence children. Remember, words can hurt, too.

2. Accentuate the Positive

Praise and reward good behavior frequently and enthusiastically. Catch children being good and compliment them on even the smallest achievements. Pay attention to the positive things they do and reward them with positive comments, treats, and privileges. Constantly nourish your child's self-esteem by showing kindness and respect.

3. Don't Sweat the Small Stuff

Ignore minor infractions, allowing a child to make mistakes. Deal with the larger problems instead. One of the characteristics of a peaceful parent is the ability to sort out what is really important in a child's behavior and to focus on it.

4. Work It Out

Make consequences a last resort. First, try to help children work out their behavior problems. Sit down with your child and try to get at the cause of his misbehavior, rather than just treating the effect. That will be more likely to prevent a reoccurrence, teach lasting lessons, and enhance the parent-child relationship. If all else fails, then consequences are in order.

5. Spare the Rod

If consequences are necessary, use the nonviolent options described in our book, such as time-out, ignoring, redirection, and taking away privileges. Remember, the type of discipline you use determines the type of a person your child will become. Peaceful discipline means teaching children positive behavior and self-control and helping them build self-esteem and important skills.

6. Pay Attention

More than half of all reported child abuse cases involve some form of neglect. You can avoid the "neglect trap" by giving lots of quality time to your children and making sure they are well taken care of when you're not at home. Neglecting a child doesn't have to mean abandoning them or not providing their daily needs. It can be as simple as not spending enough time with them or not making that time really matter.

7. Give Peace a Chance

When it comes to parenting, an old motto applies: *"If at first you don't succeed, try, try again."* Ingrained habits don't change easily. Being a peaceful parent requires time and patience. If a solution doesn't work right away, keep trying that one or another one. Eventually, you'll find a way.

8. Play It Cool

Be extra careful when you're in an angry or sad mood. It might increase your chances of hurting your child. Many parents feel like resorting to violence on occasion. The trick is to know what to do instead. With the help of professionals and books like ours, parents can learn ways to diffuse their rage before it gets out of hand.

9. Rear a Peacemaker

Peaceful parenting is more than just nonviolent discipline. It is a holistic approach that rears children to be peaceful and valuable citizens with an abundance of tolerance, understanding, compassion, and self-esteem. It teaches not only nonviolence but also social justice, equality, environmental concern, appreciation for cultural diversity, and the like. Rearing children peacefully ultimately means rearing peaceful children who will carry what they learn into the next century, assuring that nonviolence is practiced by parents of coming generations.

10. Walk the Talk

As your child's primary role model, it is important to practice what you preach. You can't expect a child to act the way you tell him or her if your own actions belie those words. If you want your children to be peaceful, you have to show them how, not just with overt actions, but in everything you do.

11. Share the Power

Create clear rules, expectations, and consequences with input from your children. Communicate them clearly and be consistent in enforcing them in a nonthreatening way that maintains self-respect. No matter how much they may resist, children need and want rules and limits. But that doesn't give parents the right to be dictators. A democratic system of decision making works better. Consistency, communication, and respect are important in enforcing rules.

Given the right amount of patience, persistence, and commitment, you can eventually achieve the intended results of peaceful child rearing. In so doing, you will eventually become more content and self-assured, less anxious about your child's behavior, and more likely to derive pleasure from the parent-child relationship. In turn, your children will gain both the immediate gratification of fulfilling rewards and the long-range benefits of proper social adjustment.

Parenting is no easy task. The many alternatives that are now available—while offering numerous options to choose from—can also lead to agonizing decision making and repeated incidents of trial-and-error. Yet, as with other kinds of hard work, child rearing can reap substantial benefits. Properly done, parenting yields innumerable rewards.

In setting out options and recommendations, we leave the ultimate decisions in your hands. We recommend that specific nonviolent choices be made. To be a parent without a child-rearing program is like being a rudderless ship in a turbulent sea. Without direction or purpose, child development is left to the risky elements of chance.

Therefore, to successfully traverse the long, often rocky road through parenting, it's necessary to begin with some goals and a specific program as the first steps toward effective child management. We hope this book has provided those initial steps.

Those of you who have come this far have taken that important first step. You have shown that you care enough about your child and yourself to seek out what is best for both of you.

Congratulations on your progress thus far. As you continue to move forward, remember that even with all you have learned up to now, you are really just beginning an exciting and significant odyssey.

CULTIVATING CHARACTER
Parent-Teacher Resources for Grades 6, 7, 8, 9, 10, 11, and 12

Richard K. Buchholz

How do you instill good character in young people? According to Richard Buchholz, you keep it simple. You get teachers and parents to work together. And you use lots of praise. With his *Cultivating Character* resource books, you use these principles to prepare young people to become good parents, workers, and citizens. Each book contains a "thought for the month" master, along with background information, that can be photocopied and posted on bulletin boards, given to students for hanging in lockers or keeping with their personal journals, and mailed to parents for posting on refrigerator doors. With constant repetition — Buchholz recommends 20 times a day — the "thought for the month" can have a powerful effect on the behavior of a young person. Simple. Easy. And effective. Memo to school administrators: the effect is cumulative and so more powerful when all grade levels participate.

EMPOWER ME!
12 Sessions for Building Self-Esteem in Girls

Helen Raica-Klotz

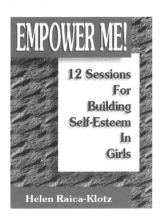

While adult women have made great strides in the past 35 years, teenage girls seem to be backsliding. They are more likely than a boy to take up smoking, to try drugs, and to get a sexually transmitted disease. *Empower Me! 12 Sessions for*

Building Self-Esteem in Girls is a manual that facilitators can use to run a self-esteem group for girls. The sessions help girls explore their individuality and improve relationships with family and friends. Because of the powerful nature of the *Empower Me!* exercises, facilitators should either be professional counselors themselves or collaborate with one.

JOURNAL ME!
A Pocketbook for Girls

Helen Raica-Klotz

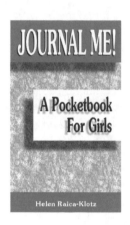

Journal Me! A Pocketbook for Girls is a short, easy-to-read guide that girls can use to explore their individuality, identify self-defeating behavior patterns, take responsibility for their feelings and actions, make better choices, and achieve happiness. The pocketbook includes simple, fun exercises and space for recording ideas, reactions, and notes. It can be used independently or as a supporting resource for *Empower Me!* sessions.

LOOKING IN, REACHING OUT
A Manual for Training Service Volunteers

Dorine and Ret Thomas

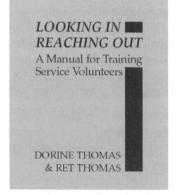

Volunteers need, and want, training. This ready-to-go training course, designed by a school counselor for service volunteers, covers all the basics. With it, you can make sure your adult or youth volunteers feel suited and prepared for helping. You can make sure they know how to listen, how to ask questions, how to identify problems, and how to make appropriate referrals. Includes handout masters with permission to photocopy. Use it as an activity book for your own meetings or as a formal training course.

SERVICE VOLUNTEER'S HANDBOOK

Dorine and Ret Thomas

Service work can be a wonderful experience for your students — when they feel properly prepared. The *Service Volunteer's Handbook* is the perfect tool to put in their hands before they go out into the field. This little book — it even fits in a pocket planner — tells students how to get organized for service, what their roles and responsibilities are, how to behave in a helping environment, how to maintain good relationships, and how to keep a positive perspective. The second half of the book covers basic skills important to service volunteers. Back matter includes client profile sheets and an address book. See also the related manual entitled *Looking In Reaching Out* by the same authors.

THE PEER HELPING TRAINING COURSE

Joan Sturkie and Maggie Phillips

Teenagers often find it easier to talk about their problems and issues with other students. And by helping teens identify and talk about their issues, peer helpers also learn something about themselves.

The Peer Helping Training Course helps teens learn how to be there for each other. The practical training course is divided into two sections. Part one (units 1–9) introduces the skills students need to be good communicators. Part two (units 10–23) deals with specific problems such as peer pressure, drugs, death, AIDS. Appendices contain a sample letter to parents of peer helpers, glossary, community resources, and an excellent bibliography.

THE PEER HELPER'S POCKETBOOK

Joan Sturkie and Valerie Gibson

Here is a small book that has proven helpful in both empowering and instructing students. It has come to symbolize responsible peer helping among students everywhere.

The Peer Helper's Pocketbook is a quick and easy guide written for peer helpers/counselors on the junior and senior high school levels as well as college. Everything needed for effective peer support is here: review of basic communication skills, counseling tips, synopsis of information on issues, and a section for important referral telephone numbers — for those times when more help is indicated. Put a copy in the faculty room because it is a handy reference for faculty, counselors, and parents.